PERGAMON INTERNATIONAL LIBRARY
of Science, Technology, Engineering and Social Studies
*The 1000-volume original paperback library in aid of education,
industrial training and the enjoyment of leisure*
Publisher: Robert Maxwell, M.C.

Cycles, Value and Employment

Responses to the Economic Crisis

THE PERGAMON TEXTBOOK
INSPECTION COPY SERVICE

An inspection copy of any book published in the Pergamon International Library will gladly be sent to academic staff without obligation for their consideration for course adoption or recommendation. Copies may be retained for a period of 60 days from receipt and returned if not suitable. When a particular title is adopted or recommended for adoption for class use and the recommendation results in a sale of 12 or more copies, the inspection copy may be retained with our compliments. The Publishers will be pleased to receive suggestions for revised editions and new titles to be published in this important International Library.

Other titles of interest

AMARA, R. and LIPINSKI, A. J.
Business Planning for an Uncertain Future

GIARINI, O.
Dialogue on Wealth and Welfare

GIARINI, O. and LOUBERGE, H.
The Diminishing Returns of Technology

LASZLO, E.
The Inner Limits of Mankind

PECCEI, A.
The Human Quality

A related journal

ECONOMIC BULLETIN FOR EUROPE
The Journal of the United Nations Economic Commission for Europe
Edited by United Nations Economic Commission for Europe, Palais des Nations, Geneva 10, Switzerland

The Bulletin is one of the foremost European economic publications. It publishes studies on contemporary economic problems affecting Europe and North America in the context of the world economy. It reflects the full range of topics addressed by the UNECE in its economic research programmes and is particularly noted for its studies of East–West economic relations.

Cycles, Value and Employment

Responses to the Economic Crisis

Edited by
ORIO GIARINI

PERGAMON PRESS
OXFORD · NEW YORK · TORONTO · SYDNEY · PARIS · FRANKFURT

U.K.	Pergamon Press Ltd., Headington Hill Hall, Oxford OX3 0BW, England
U.S.A.	Pergamon Press Inc., Maxwell House, Fairview Park, Elmsford, New York 10523, U.S.A.
CANADA	Pergamon Press Canada Ltd., Suite 104, 150 Consumers Road, Willowdale, Ontario M2J 1P9, Canada
AUSTRALIA	Pergamon Press (Aust.) Pty. Ltd., P.O. Box 544, Potts Point, N.S.W. 2011, Australia
FRANCE	Pergamon Press SARL, 24 rue des Ecoles, 75240 Paris, Cedex 05, France
FEDERAL REPUBLIC OF GERMANY	Pergamon Press GmbH, Hammerweg 6, D-6242 Kronberg-Taunus, Federal Republic of Germany

Copyright © 1984 Orio Giarini

All Rights Reserved. No part of this publication may be reproduced, stored in a retrieval system or transmitted in any form or by any means: electronic, electrostatic, magnetic tape, mechanical, photocopying, recording or otherwise, without permission in writing from the publishers.

First edition 1984

Library of Congress Cataloging in Publication Data
Main entry under title:
Cycles, value, and employment.
(Pergamon international library of science, technology, engineering, and social studies)
1. Business cycles—Addresses, essays, lectures.
2. Long waves (Economics)—Addresses, essays, lectures. 3. Technological innovations——Addresses, essays, lectures. 4. Economic policy—Addresses, essays, lectures. I. Giarini, Orio. II. Series.
HB3711.C93   1984   339.5   84–6170

British Library Cataloguing in Publication Data
Cycles, value and employment.—(Pergamon international library)
1. Business cycles 2. Technological innovations
I. Giarini, Orio
338.5'42   HB3711
ISBN 0-08-031284-5 (Hardcover)
ISBN 0-08-031283-7 (Flexicover)

Printed in Great Britain by A. Wheaton & Co. Ltd., Exeter

Contents

1. **The Long-Term Economic Movements and the Dynamics of Technical Progress: Their Implications for a Policy of Science, Technology and Scientific Developments**   1
   by Orio Giarini and Henri Loubergé

   1. The Macro-cycle, or the Kondratieff Movement   4
   2. The Life Cycle of the Industrial Revolution   17
   3. The Dynamics of Technical Progress in the Contemporary Economy   29

   References   40

2. **The Notion of Economic Value in the Post-Industrial Society: Factors in the Search for New Economic Paradigms**   41

3. **Notes**   67

   The Employment Problem   68
   A New "Supply Side" Economics: The Question of "The Diminishing Returns of Technology"   75
   Economic Crisis, Interest Rates and the Diminishing Returns of Technology   77

Index   81

1

The Long-Term Economic Movements and the Dynamics of Technical Progress: Their Implications for a Policy of Science, Technology and Scientific Developments*

by

Orio Giarini and Henri Loubergé

In all the industrialised countries the 1970s have been characterised by a substantial decrease in the average growth rate. This has been limited to 2 or 3%, while since the end of the 1940s we have been accustomed to average growth rates of the order of 6%.

During the period 1973–1977 the general opinion was that the economic difficulties were of a coincidental nature. For most economists, the fall in investment and the increase in unemployment reflected the uncertainty of economic agents faced with the increase in the oil price. It was proper for the State to intervene with budgetary and monetary policies to revive demand, to relaunch the economy and thus re-establish the confidence of managers and investors.

The danger of this intervention is today apparent since it has led to an increase in inflation (which had already reached a worrying level at the beginning of the 1970s) and high public borrowing. The policy is widely discredited, except in certain countries, corresponding to the fact that the coincidental vision of the situation has given place to a more structural view. Given the ineffectiveness of the corrective actions undertaken, it became obvious that there is today a fundamental tendency for economic activity to slow down and that the oil crisis was only a symptom of this tendency.

---

* Report written at the request of Societe Internationale des Conseillers de Synthese on behalf of the General Management of Science, Research and Development of the Commission of the European Communities (Programme Fast).

2   Cycles, Value and Employment

It should be noted that a growth rate of about 2 to 3% is about the average of the economic development over the last two centuries, that is since the beginning of the industrial revolution. From a very broad historical perspective, one is thus tempted to reverse the reasoning and to see in the present situation a return to normal after a period of exceptional economic growth, from 1945 to 1973.

This realisation has naturally caused a renewal of interest in the hypothesis of long-term economic movements, and particularly in Kondratieff's theory of cycles. According to this theory, economic activity is subject to long-term oscillations (of the order of 50-year wavelengths) in which tendencies to strong economic growth and a slowing down of economic activity alternate. If this were true, the actual economic situation could be validly interpreted as an historic downturn period, destined to last until about 1990, after a development period from approximately 1940 to 1970.

Such an hypothesis is all the more interesting when linked to the following observation: never in the past has there been the number of talented workers engaged in fundamental research and active technicians in applied research comparable with the number which we have today. Nevertheless, even if we have constant technological progress, this does not seem to have a great effect on economic activity. Now the main explanation of long-term movements turns on the variations in intensity of technical progress. Following this reasoning a little further, one could then see that the present economic crisis is the result of a lack of fundamental innovations, and that to remedy this state of affairs, we must try to increase government assistance for the development of relevant technologies.

With these considerations in mind, the present work is meant to provide preliminary points of reference for a more systematic study of long-term economic evolution. It consists of three chapters.

The first chapter comprises an analysis of the economic literature on long-term economic cycles; the original contribution of Kondratieff (1926), different interpretations (particularly those of Schumpeter (1939), Dupriez (1951) and Forrester (1977)), and later verifications (particularly Garvy (1943) and Bossier and Hugé (1981)). The conclusion is that there seem not to be regular economic cycles, but that one cannot disprove the hypothesis of there being different development phases since the beginning of the industrial revolution.

The second chapter has to do with the historical analysis of these phases of development and their economic interpretation, developing work by Landes (1972), Mandel (1980), and Giarini and Loubergé (1978). They give evidence for the existence of two waves of technological progress over the last two centuries, and analyse the dynamics and the economic potential of technical progress in the contemporary historical situation.

Finally the third chapter presents the results of a study carried out within the areas of industry and research. From this we attempt to build up a picture of the dynamics of technical progress over the period 1750 to 2000. It proposes, in conclusion, several principles of orientation of economic policy, particularly as regards research and technology.

CHAPTER 1

The Macro-cycle, or the Kondratieff Movement

1. The Kondratieff Contribution

The idea of a long-term economic movement is generally associated with the name of the Russian economist Nikolai D. Kondratieff.* Born in 1892, he became after the Bolshevik Revolution a Professor at the Agriculture Academy and Director of the Institute of Research into Organisation in Moscow. His theory on long-term cycles was developed from 1922. They were published in an article appearing in 1926 in *Archiv für Sozialwissenschaft und Sozialpolitik,* and in 1935 in *The Review of Economics and Statistics.* The theory gave rise to a wide debate in the Soviet Union during the 1920s, but it was finally judged "false and reactionary" by the official Soviet Encyclopedia in 1929 (according to Garvy, 1943). In 1930, Kondratieff was arrested and deported to Siberia. In the *Gulag Archipelago,* Solzhenitsyn (1974) mentions his presence in different camps during the 1930s. He probably died in one of these, at an unknown date.

Kondratieff's theory is based on the statistical analysis of time series of several variables (prices, interest rates, business, the production of coal and raw materials) in different countries (Germany, France, England and the United States mainly). He gave evidence for three large long-term oscillations: the first movement lasted approximately 60 years (from 1790 to 1850, peaking between 1810 and 1817). The second lasted about 45 years (from 1850 to 1895, with the top of the cycle about 1875). The third, beginning about 1895, attained its peak between 1914 and 1920.

In spite of this, Kondratieff remained relatively careful about the general impact of his theory, as the following passage shows, taken from his 1935 article (page 112):

> "The relevant data which we were able to quote cover about 140 years. This period comprises two and one-half cycles only. Although the period embraced by the data is sufficient to decide the question of the existence of long waves, it is not enough to enable us to assert

---

* This association is due to Schumpeter (1939). For Kondratieff's predecessors, see Eklund (1980).

beyond doubt the cyclical character of those waves. Nevertheless we believe that the available data is sufficient to declare this cyclical character to be very probable."

He had nevertheless given an essential push to economic thought, a push which translated into two waves of curiosity about long-term movements: the first at the beginning of the 1940s; the second at the end of the 1970s. In each of these periods there has been investigation both of the reality of these cycles and of their causes.

2. Characteristics and Causes of the Kondratieff Cycle

The adherents of Kondratieff's theory agree quite well on the description of the general state of the economy in each of the two phases of the cycle, the expansionary phase and the contractionary phase. Kondratieff himself had already described certain characteristics of the cycle which bears his name:

> During the expansionary phase, the years of prosperity are more numerous, while they become less common in a contraction.
> At the beginning of the expansion, we see an increase in production of gold and an expansion of world markets.
> The most deadly wars occur during the expansion.
> Contraction is accompanied by substantial progress in the technical domain, but the passage from invention to innovation occurs only in an upturn.

Table 1 presents views of different authors on the principal characteristics

TABLE 1. *The principal economic and social characteristics in each phase of the macro-cycle*

Expansion	Decline
• Inflation develops	• Deflation predominates
• The years of prosperity are more frequent than years of depression or recession	• Years of prosperity are less frequent
• Profits are high	• Profits are low and bankruptcies increase
• Technological innovations are numerous	• Entrepreneurship seems weak
• Strong incentives to invest	• Lack of investment
• Unemployment is only an incidental problem	• Structural unemployment develops
• Government budget deficits	• Government budget surplus
• Opening of external markets	• Increase in protectionism
• High social tension, demands and social problems	• Relative apathy in the social domain
• Optimism, aggression, artistic creativity	• Pessimism, lessening of cultural activities
• Violent wars	• Relatively less violent wars

of the economic and social situation in each phase of the macro-cycle. One could add to it the opinion of Shuman and Rosenau (1972) for whom the period at the peak of the cycle is a happy time, a time of prosperity without inflation, and a disappearance of social tensions which had arisen during the expansionary phase.

On the other hand, opinions diverge when it comes to examining the causes of the long cycle. Some authors have tried to explain them by non-economic forces, mainly military conflicts and demographic changes. But it hardly seems wise to separate these phenomena from their economic context. One can consider that they are attributable to the general economic trend represented by Kondratieff's phases (several authors, starting with Kondratieff, have subscribed to this idea). One can also agree with Dupriez (1951) that "economic movements and conflicts are part of a wider and hence looser social process, at the heart of which several patterns recur" (page 242).

It is preferable then to keep to economic explanations, which in any case are quite varied.

A. Absence of Opinion

It is perhaps worthwhile to mention that some authors are more or less disinterested in the problem. This is the case of Shuman and Rosenau (1972), who have nonetheless devoted a book to the theme of the Kondratieff cycle:

> "There seems to be no rational basis for the upswing of the long wave any more than there is for the downswing. (...) The periodicity of the entire wave is puzzling. (...) Even more difficult to understand is why the reversal should come at a predictable time" (pp. 76–77).

This is also the case for Kondratieff himself, who seems more interested in the correlations that he observes between the macro-cycle and phenomena such as the spread of technical progress, gold discoveries, wars and revolutions. On the problem of the causes of the cycle, he could not be more vague:

> "Long waves arise out of causes which are inherent in the essence of the capitalist economy" (1935, p. 115).

One point, that is all.

B. The Role of Innovation

The most famous explanation is that given by Schumpeter (1939). It has received the support of Imbert (1959) and has recently been reconsidered and shored up by Mensch (1977).

For Schumpeter, the Kondratieff movements, as for other cycles of shorter duration, have their origin in the creative power of the spirit of the firm. They are the fundamental waves of innovation in the industrial sector which place the economy on an increasing trend. These innovations entail a strong demand for capital goods, a lowering of production costs and the launching of new products. Thus there is at the same time an increase in demand (through the multiplier effect of investments and creation of new consumption needs) and an increase in capacity on the supply side, so that output can grow, profits accumulate, unemployment disappear, etc. The initial stimulating effect of these fundamental innovations has been followed by less important innovations which allow the extension of the growing phase, but at a decreasing momentum. The turning of the cycle happens because of the excess investment which occurred during the prosperous years. In a market economy, such excesses are accompanied by economic losses, bankruptcies and lay-offs. This gives the necessary push to a cumulative movement towards crisis which lasts until the overcapitalisation and the overindebtedness of the economy have disappeared. The path is then clear for the spirit of the firm to re-surface and for a new wave of innovations to begin another cycle.

Historically, Schumpeter links the three Kondratieff cycles of the period 1750–1940 to the three waves of fundamental innovations in the following economic branches: textiles and iron at the end of the eighteenth century; transport (railways) in the middle of the nineteenth century; and electricity, chemistry and transport (automobiles) at the beginning of the twentieth century. If one accepts the hypothesis of a fourth Kondratieff cycle in the middle of the twentieth century, the origin must be the fundamental innovations in energy sources (oil research), transport (aeroplanes) and electronics (computers).

Mensch (1977) has put flesh on the Schumpeterian bones (see Fig. 1), but he has also proceeded to develop the ideas outlined above, particularly as regards the causes of the cycle turning. For him, the problem arises from a breakdown in the transmission of knowledge during the expansion. The firms' energies are thus absorbed by the problems of their development, and they hasten to profit from the opportunities offered in a period when all seems possible. Therefore, they neglect scientific research which, however, is the basis of all processes of production of innovations. Now, once the effects of initial innovations have worn off, it is too late to develop new technologies because this takes time. The seeking of maximum short-term profit encourages them to neglect risky innovations requiring substantial investment (Basisinnovationen) and to prefer false innovations (Scheininnovationen), which have no motor effect on the economy. It is

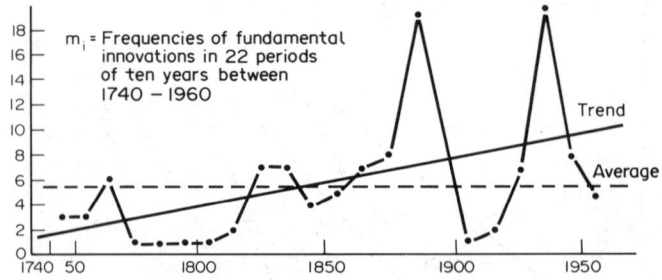

FIG. 1. *Number of fundamental innovations during each of the 22 decades during the period 1740–1960.*
(Source: Mensch (1977), p. 142.)

only when the crisis has become acute that the entrepreneurs need to look for new products and carry out research on new processes.

Mensch's study in its turn has been the object of further refinement on the part of Marchetti (1980), who used the statistical material gathered together by Mensch to study the characteristics of each of the innovatory waves shown in Fig. 1 in greater detail. He was able to show that, as each cycle advances, the delay between invention (at the level of fundamental research) and innovation (at the level of industrial development) shrinks. On the other hand, it expands again when one jumps from the end of one cycle to the beginning of the following cycle. This phenomenon is shown in Fig. 2. This figure also allows us to see that there is some acceleration of development phases. The cumulative percentage of innovations appearing during the first cycle passed from 10% to 90% in 47 years, while this occurrence needed 33 years and 23 years for the second and third cycles. Marchetti gives no explanation for this phenomenon, but one can probably attribute it to a learning effect: from one cycle to the next, entrepreneurs better realise the impact which innovation can have on their profits, and they learn to take more rapid advantage of the opportunities offered by research and development.

Nevertheless, the graph does not allow us to corroborate the claims of Marchetti on a link between the start of one innovatory phase and the appearance of a new energy source, the utilisation of which would last until the epicentre of the following cycle. Oil does not completely fit this model, for its production cycle is too short. Besides, such a model depends strongly on the assumptions made on the future utilisation of alternative energy sources.

On the basis of the results shown in Fig. 2, Marchetti has the temerity to predict the characteristics of the next cycle. His predictions are given in Figure 3. The epicentre of the fourth invention–innovation wave appears in 1980, coinciding with the peak of the production cycle of oil. The

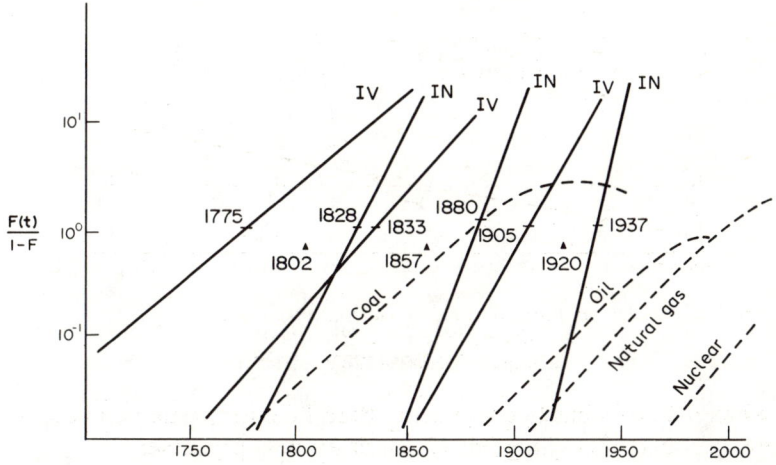

FIG. 2. *Waves of invention (IV) and innovation (IN)*. F(t) *represents the cumulative proportion of the total of the inventions (innovations) of the wave at time* t. F/(1-F) *is measured on a logarithmic scale.*
(Source: Marchetti: Society as a Learning System, in *Technological Forecasting and Social Change*, **18**, 1980, p. 279).

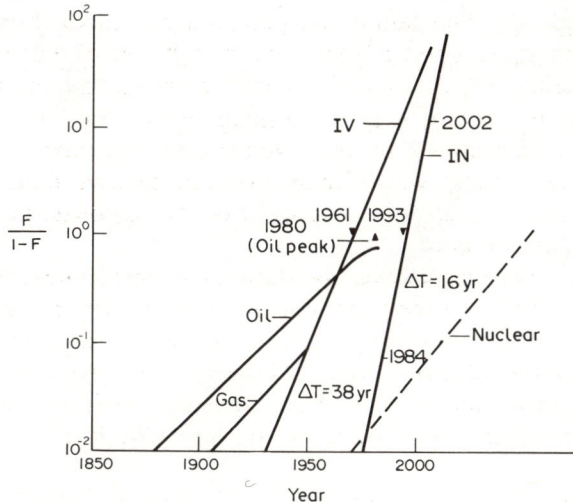

FIG. 3. *Waves of invention (IV) and innovation (IN).*
(Source: Marchetti: Society as a Learning System, in *Technological Forecasting and Society Change*, **18**, 1980, p. 279).

essential characteristic inventions of this wave occur in the period 1950–1985, while the crucial period of appearance of new innovations is the 16 years between 1984 and 2000, which happens to correspond with the predictions previously made by Mensch. According to Marchetti, this fourth wave of innovations would be accompanied by intensive use of natural gas and increasing use of nuclear energy.

There certainly exist many pertinent ideas in the models which link the Kondratieff movement with innovation. The most pertinent of all are those explaining historical discontinuities by changes in technical progress (Fig. 1). But the explanations put forward are not totally convincing.

Schumpeter's theory is basically that of fluctuations in entrepreneurial spirit, rather than a theory of innovatory cycles. In the Schumpeterian model, there are no discontinuities in technological potential. It is the general economic conditions which sometimes cause the appearance of a wave of innovations, and sometimes block this wave. This foreshadows other explanations, given below, in which technical progress is instead an endogenous factor. There remains, however, to discover what causes the fluctuations in entrepreneurial spirit.

Mensch's explanation, taken up by Marchetti, is more precise, but also more problematical. It is difficult to believe that entrepreneurs will disregard the possibility of high profits in an economic boom period, and be content with their limited but sure profit, other things being equal. More complex economic and social phenomena would seem to enter into the decision of whether or not to innovate.

As for the rest, the assertion that entrepreneurs neglect research during the expansionary phase has not been proved. On the contrary, by using the statistical tables presented by Mensch and Marchetti, it is possible to cast serious doubt on the hypothesis of very marked fluctuations in the frequency of inventions. Thus, in Fig. 4, in which the dotted line gives the chronological evolution of the frequency of innovations, while the solid line superimposed on it shows the frequency of inventions, there appears a

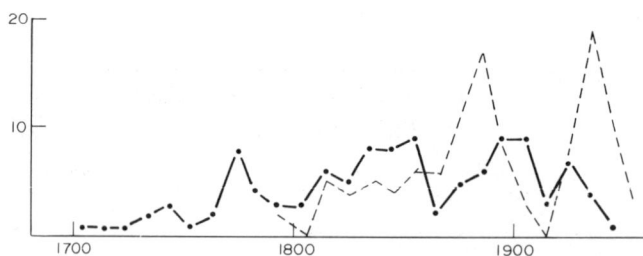

FIG. 4. *Number of fundamental inventions (solid line) compared with the corresponding number of fundamental innovations (dotted line).*
(Source: Mensch (1977)).

clear difference in amplitude between the fluctuations of the two curves. The invention phenomenon is less irregular than the innovation phenomenon. We are thus led back to Schumpeter's thesis and to this fundamental question: why is the attraction of innovation less in some periods than in others?

C. The Life Cycle of Capital

Forrester's model (1977 and 1978) is an extension of Schumpeter's. Forrester does not deny the existence of discontinuities in the occurrence of innovations, but he considers them the effect of a more fundamental cause: the periodic replacement of a large proportion of capital. This phenomenon has nothing to do with any obsolescence caused by technical progress. It is merely due to the natural life cycle of capital and it means that investment slackens every 40 or 50 years. In a depression, the lowering of the demand for capital depresses all of the economy and it encourages managers to shelve innovatory projects. This causes the periods of technological slack and a reserve of un-utilised inventions. During a boom, on the other hand, the replacement of capital is the time to appeal to the latest technical developments and one sees a flowering of new technologies to some extent everywhere. There is simultaneously a growth period and a period in which the entrepreneurs make massive use of technical progress, but this technical progress does not play any role as an economic motor. In the limit, long-term economic movements would occur even if technical progress did not exist. And this is precisely what happens in the dynamic model used by Forrester to simulate the American economy's long-term evolution. The model does not incorporate technical progress, but it makes macro-cycles appear, caused only by the action of delays in the investment sector: "A long wave is being created without technological change" (1977, p. 539).

Here again one can be dubious. First, Forrester's thesis has not so far been supported by a statistical study. It rests merely on *ad hoc* remarks. Now if one examines this model, it seems that 40 or 50 years represents a very long period for the life cycle of capital. Further, it seems unrealistic to suppose that investment is completely independent of new technological possibilities. It would suffice for a single entrepreneur to decide not to wait to renew his capital, that he takes advantage of an important innovation to change his machinery, and all of Forrester's theoretical construction flounders: if technical progress really allows the lowering of costs, the other entrepreneurs must follow more or less quickly or go bankrupt. Finally, Forrester's conception of technical progress is too narrow. Innovation does not just exist for capital goods of firms. It also exists in the creation of new products and in the discovery of new sources of energy. There is potential here for de-stabilising events which would turn economic reality on its head and which do not enter into the Forrester framework of regular cycles. The invention of the motor-car, of television, etc., constitute major phenomena, and yet these phenomena are not accounted for in the model described above.

D. Monetary Factors

In the research into the causes of the Kondratieff cycle, monetary factors have received particular attention by Dupriez (1951, 1959). His judgement is rather subtle, because while he accords monetary movements an important place, he does not hide the fact that these should not be considered as the only source of the macro-cycle. His idea is that there exists a set of factors which interact and which make the economy evolve along a long-term track, in one direction or the other:

> "The central phenomenon is a change in the money–goods ratio, caused by the absence, in one sense or another, of regulatory mechanisms in this matter. (...) The changes in the money–goods ratio is not attributable, as has often been thought, only to monetary causes; social phenomena have had a growing influence, wars having particularly caused pronounced deflationary attitudes and important transformations of monetary institutions" (1951, p. 275).

Dupriez attaches some importance to fluctuations in the supply of precious metals, and the amplification which these receive through credit instruments, but he is above all sensitive to the attitude of the popular masses and their rulers towards money. Changes in attitude according to him are caused by large movements in the demand function for money and by monetary reforms which generate tendentious movements in the real sector of the economy. On the contrary, technical progress is a phenomenon which transcends these long movements. It occurs in a general movement of economic expansion which one counts in centuries rather than in decades.

In the final analysis, however, Dupriez's analysis leaves something to be desired, because he finds no clear reason for changes in monetary behaviour. The enormous work in the statistical analysis which Dupriez has given does not bring a definite response to the questions on the causes of the Kondratieff cycle. Dupriez himself finishes by concluding that the search for a specific cause is hopeless (1959, p. 253). From there it is a short step to consider the macro-cycle as a risky phenomenon, and thus to reconsider its importance. Several authors have been eager to take this step.

3. Does the Kondratieff Cycle Really Exist?

The theory of long cycles has been subject to lively criticism, particularly at the beginning of the 1940s, which has led to its almost complete disappearance from economic debates until very recently. Thus, in Samuelson's book (1972), it is merely the subject of a note at the bottom of a page (p. 363).

The destructive character of the criticisms can be explained in part by ideological reasons. The hypothesis of a regular Kondratieff cycle presupposes the existence of an historic determinism, a close relative of the Marxist philosophy of history, which plays down human liberty and the possibilities of radically influencing the course of events through rational decisions. It is therefore subject to an *a priori* rebuttal on the part of all those who do not share this vision of history. Most of the time, this rebuttal is implicit, but it is also sometimes clearly expressed, as in the following passage, taken from Maguire's (1981) article:

> "The Kondratieff models and their offshoots are dangerous for a leader because they stress certainty and reaction, hence reducing the role which an individual can play to influence his future. Now the certainty that the individual is capable of exercising some control over his environment, that he can act on his own destiny, that he is, at least up to a certain point, in a position to model his own future should be at the heart of every leader's actions. This is why the mechanistic models are simply unacceptable for decision makers in industrialised countries of the West" (p. 93).

However, ideological reasons do not suffice to explain the doubts expressed about the works of Kondratieff, Schumpeter, and others. There exist also objective reasons for criticism.

The attack on Kondratieff comes first from his own compatriot, Trotsky. In the West, it has principally been the work of Garvy (1943) which analysed the statistical methods used by Kondratieff and the interpretation of his results, especially as regards the regularity of the observed movements.

The analytical procedure used by Kondratieff seems in fact to be lacking in several ways, particularly because he did not smooth time series in a consistent manner. As for the results, they are a long way from having the meaning which Kondratieff ascribes to them. The series in question do in fact show long-term movements, but these movements disappear when the series are expressed in real terms.

This leads Garvy to conclude with these words:

> "Our analysis shows that the existence of long swings could not be proved in the production series studied by Kondratieff; that data for

all four major capitalist countries and the two series with world-wide coverage pertain only to one cycle; that, consequently, neither the international character of the phenomenon nor its recurrence at regular time intervals can be ascertained by the material presented" (Garvy, 1943, p. 219).

The treatment of Schumpeter is hardly less severe. Schumpeter thought that the structural changes in the economy over the two centuries since the industrial revolution invalidated any analysis based exclusively on statistical treatment of time series data. Thus he preferred to appeal broadly to the qualitative interpretation of historical experience. But having done this, he exposed himself to the criticism of having proved nothing. His model can be considered as a working hypothesis, shored up by arguments and examples, but it could not provide a convincing explanation of reality for those who are not impressed with the theory of long term cycles. Whence the virulent criticism by Kuznets:

"The three-cycle schema and the rather rigid relationship claimed to have been established among the three groups of cycles (i.e. Kondratieff, Juglar and Kitchin) cannot be considered, on the basis of the evidence submitted, even tolerably valid; nor could such validity be established without a serviceable statistical procedure" (Kuznets, 1940, p. 270; mentioned by Eklund, 1980, p. 395).

Overall, if one looks at the statistical evidence, one single thing is clear: there was during the period 1780–1940 a long-term movement in prices with apparent cycles, and with a period of about 50 years (see Fig. 5). But on the one hand this movement seems to have disappeared in the 1950s to give rise to a continuous wave of inflation; and on the other hand the

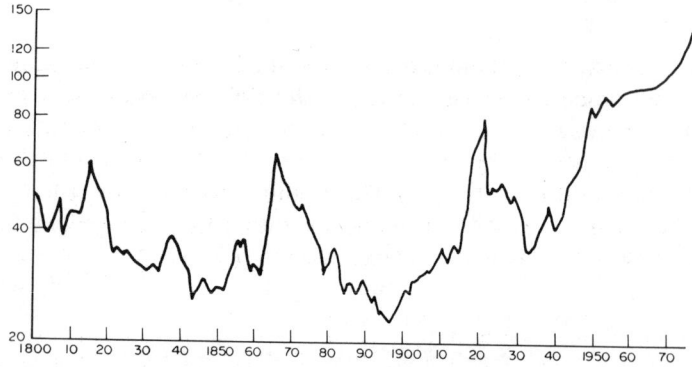

FIG. 5. *Wholesale price index in the U.S. 1800–1974.*
(Source: Eklund, 1980, p. 399).

inflationary points around the years 1815, 1865 and 1915–1920, can be easily explained by historical factors: wars and discoveries of gold mines.

In fact, the movements shown in Fig. 5 seem to correspond perfectly to a model of historical evolution which is more global and less mechanical than that of the Kondratieff cycles.

This model is the following (see Landes, 1972):

— In the course of the nineteenth century, technical progress, the spread of the industrial revolution, and freedom of competition have caused the appearance of a deflationary trend. This tendentious movement has however been interrupted by "accidents" (wars and discoveries of precious metals).
— Since the beginning of the twentieth century, changes in the economic and social structure have caused the appearance of an inflationary trend. Movements above this trend correspond to increases in the money supply after the war of 1914–1918, and movements below this trend correspond to the brutal deflationary reaction of the monetary authorities over the 1920s.

As for long-term production changes, it is not possible to affirm that they exist. The rare empirical studies which have tackled this problem over the last years, and which have all used techniques of spectral analysis (Adelman, 1965;* Dowling and Poulson, 1974; Bossier and Hugé, 1981) have not drawn any definite conclusions. Periodic movements cannot be completely disregarded, but they seem irregular, and one can attribute them either to factors of uncertainty,† or to distortions introduced by techniques of smoothing time series.

We are thus led to reject the hypothesis of a regular Kondratieff cycle. Nevertheless it still remains true that the economic growth seen since the end of the eighteenth century has not been regular. As Weinstock (1964, p. 102), writes:

> "Since the exact, mathematical form of the long wave is not successful, one must discard the classification of different periods, with their differing characteristics, under a single grouping (generally on the basis of quantitative historical data), and resolve to treat each period more or less differently. (...) This means, however, that long waves must be regarded as 'historical epochs' rather than 'true cycles'. (...) A succession of trends is the result, not a long wave."

---

* More specifically, this study treats the cycles of Kuznets, with a period of about 20 years, which were observed in the U.S. until the 1914–1918 war, and which can be linked with immigration phenomena.

† Forrester (1977) notes that weak, random shocks are sufficient to create and maintain a cyclical movement.

The hypothesis of long-term cycles gives way to an hypothesis of discontinuities in the development rhythm of the western economies. Rather than work with an oscillatory movement one must work within the structure of a civilisation cycle (cycle here being taken in the sense of life cycle) stretching over several centuries. The observations of economic and social order which authors such as Schumpeter have tried to insert into the theoretical framework of long-term cycles, and more particularly those observations which have to do with the innovatory rhythm, can thus be reinterpreted as adjustment phenomena relative to the trend of the civilisation cycle.

This hypothesis, which is often presented when concluding studies on the Kondratieff cycle (see Garvy, Imbert, Weinstock, Forrester, Eklund), is the point of departure for the following chapter.

CHAPTER 2

The Life Cycle of the Industrial Revolution

Having rejected the hypothesis of irregular Kondratieff cycles, ineluctably ordering the progress of industrial economies, there remains to investigate the causes of the indisputable variations in intensity of long-term economic development. It is necessary to examine under a different light the phenomena which formed the subject matter of the studies discussed in the preceding chapter. Instead of seeking to infer, from the observation of these phenomena, a mechanical law of long-term evolution, it seems better to reintroduce a certain amount of uncertainty to proceed to a qualitative analysis of historical reality.

Taking account of thinking on contemporary economic problems, this attitude places rather greater stress on freedom of decision. It does not view the future as predetermined. It aims rather to furnish an interpretative framework for the analysis of the difficulties encountered and for the selection of policies able to overcome these difficulties.

When studying the historical developments of the western economy, one cannot ignore Marxist analysis. This in fact offers an interpretative model which goes some way towards forming a coherent response to all the principal phenomena of capitalist production, and the changes in rhythm of the growth of the economy is no exception to the rule. This is why we shall first present the Marxist hypothesis before giving a non-Marxist hypothesis, stressing the variations of quality in scientific and technical process.

1. The Marxist Explanation

The best Marxist explanation of long-term economic movements has been given by Mandel (1980). Like many other authors, Mandel rejects the hypothesis of regular Kondratieff cycles. He admits that the economic laws of behaviour can explain the passage from a period of economic prosperity to one of depression. According to him, this passage simply reflects the tendency for the profit rate to decrease, followed by an increase in the organic composition of capital (that is, the appropriate capital labour ratio). On the other hand, he maintains that no economic law can explain the rebirth of the capitalist economy at the end of a depression. In his opinion, this re-awakening can only be caused by non-economic factors allowing an increase in the rate of profit. These factors are three in number:

> The increase in surplus value, following a social defeat of the working class;
> The lowering of the growth rate of the organic composition of capital, due to an extension of the capitalist methods of production in pre-industrial zones;
> The acceleration of the replacement of capital, followed by substantial technical progress in the areas of transport, telecommunications and credit.

Mandel thinks that the three historic phases of re-starting economy activity, which took place respectively in 1848, 1893 and 1940, are entirely due to these three factors. In 1848, it was particularly the second factor which was important, with the spread of the industrial revolution into central Europe and the United States. It was the second and third factors in 1893: the colonisation of Africa, the Middle East and Asia, the steamship, the telegraph, the extension of the railway network, the development of limited liability companies, of credit, and of large shops were the determinant phenomena. Finally in 1940 the first factor caused the qualitative jump. Fascism, the World War and the Cold War created the necessary conditions for the will to fight of the working class to recede and for an increase in the rate of surplus value.

The Marxist theory of long movements thus associates these movements with the succession of different phases in the class struggle, which allows capitalism to regain the initiative, and retards its demise.

Although Mandel introduces certain changes, to do with political and social factors, in the causes of the resurgence of capitalism, he does not give innovations in general a key role in the renewal mechanism. In his eyes, groups of innovations constitute an endogenous phenomenon, depending on the variations in the average profit rate. They accentuate the take-off, but they do not cause it:

> "We have said that although the key turning points are clearly brought about by exogenous extraeconomic factors, they unleash dynamic processes that can then be explained by the inner logic of the capitalist laws of motion. It is at this point that we attribute an important role to technological revolutions, as did Marx himself. (...) Large-scale innovation does not take place during the long wave of relative stagnation that precedes a technological revolution because profit

expectations are mediocre. Precisely for that reason, once the sharp upsurge in the rate of profit starts, capital finds a reserve of unapplied or only marginally applied inventions and therefore has the material wherewithal for an upsurge in the rate of technological innovation. When a basic technological revolution occurs, this in itself is already of long duration" (Mandel, 1980, pp. 24–25).

On the contrary, when the law of the decreasing tendency of the profit rate comes into full swing, the incentive to innovate decreases, investments stop, and the crisis in the economic process begins. According to Mandel, this is the explanation of the general slowing down of economic growth since 1968: the willingness of the working class to struggle, the retreat of imperialism and the increase in the organic composition of capital have led to a fall in the profit rate and the "technological stalemate" of which Mensch speaks. Still according to Mandel, these problems actually lead to a period of social and political renewal destined to weaken trade union power and to create conditions for an increase in the average rate of profits. The outcome of this situation, however, is uncertain because the marriage of convenience between capitalists and workers is far less favourable to the former than in comparable episodes in the past. Thus one should fear the worst for the future, i.e. the outcome that the actual economic crisis leads to massive unemployment, to wars and to violent revolutions.

If one evaluates Mandel's thesis, in some respects it seems very attractive for our purposes. It rejects mechanical theories of long-term cycles and substitutes for them an analysis of economic development in an historical context. Besides, it gives an acceptable explanation of the phenomenon of innovatory waves, linking these to the entrepreneurs' prospects of profits.

On the debit side, we must mention the fact that his thesis places the analysis of the life cycle of the industrial revolution in the framework of a very long-term determinism. The class struggle is in fact the motive element of long period movements. If nothing else happens, each period of depression in the capitalist society leads inevitably to a reaction on the part of the beneficiaries of the profits and thus to a period of social and political tensions. The outcome of each of these periods is uncertain, but the outcome of the process itself is not: socialism will necessarily be introduced. The resurgences of capitalism cannot recur indefinitely.

This is where it seems necessary to cast a different, non-Marxist, light on the life cycle of the industrial revolution. The long-term movement can in fact also be explained in a more classical framework, in which historical breaks occur because of qualitative modifications in scientific and technical development and not only because of political and social factors.

20   *Cycles, Value and Employment*

2. The Two Technological Waves of the Industrial Revolution

In what follows, the analysis has to do with the evolution of the fundamental economic structure over the period 1750–1980.

Our point of departure is two widely admitted postulates:

> (i) the industrial revolution which took place, first in Great Britain in the eighteenth century, then spread to the European and North American continents in the nineteenth century, represents a very important break in human history. It is the point of departure of a period of unprecedented economic growth, which has allowed Western countries to move from economies still characterised by the existence of chronic famines to an economy of abundance.
>
> (ii) Technical progress has played an essential role in the development of the industrial revolution.

When, starting from these two postulates, one examines more closely the role and nature of technical progress, one notices that the conditions under which technical progress influences the level of production have considerably changed since the eighteenth century. More precisely, the industrial revolution of the eighteenth century was based on a type of technical progress qualitatively different from that which we know today, which had begun to emerge at the end of the nineteenth century.

In fact, the industrial revolution of the eighteenth century was characterised by the use, on a bigger scale, of a technology which had existed from the time of the first man and which consisted of using materials and constructing tools by utilising the direct perception of our senses. The fundamental innovation of the steam engine was based on the observation that water, by producing steam, increases its volume. This increase in volume produces pressure which one can utilise in a mechanical fashion, and all this without needing any "scientific" knowledge of the structure of water or of the resistive capacity of the containers which were built to hold this steam.

It was essentially the steam engine which led the weaver to depart from his country house and to establish an autonomous unit of production, namely a factory. Thus began an irreversible process of concentration of industrial production, which profoundly changed the economic structure by dissociating industry and agriculture.

More generally though, it is important to note that the industrial revolution was linked with the appearance of economic human and political conditions, so much so that traditional inventions gave birth to industrial innovations producing productivity gains, and hence a lowering in the relative price of manufactured goods.

This scenario was changed from the end of the nineteenth century. Even if the traditional technology continued to develop (it still continues to do so today) we have seen the appearance of a different type of technology, based on scientific knowledge. Thanks to progress in the natural sciences and in education, one began to realise that scientific research could be applied to the resolution of specific industrial problems. Better still, the stock of new scientific knowledge accumulated since the time of Descartes and Newton was a source from which the engineer and entrepreneur could, if they had the idea to do so, draw new inspirations to put new processes into effect and to introduce new products on to the market.

This process is very well described in the work of Landes (1972). The importance of this work is to have realised the notion of scientific discovery. This is not a more or less modern method which was applied to the technology of the period of the industrial revolution. It is a quite different thing: it is the end product of the philosophy which wished to verify its search for knowledge of matter and of the universe by experimentation. Thus, through Physics, Chemistry, Biology and all the other scientific fields, one began to know the materials and the structures of the universe, the biggest as well as the smallest, at a level which is no longer naturally perceptible by a human being. It no longer suffices to experience an environment through our senses, but intermediary sciences must be developed which allow us to know the structure of matter to the point of being able to manipulate it. Thus the old technology could use cotton or the wool fibres which were already provided as such by nature, but the knowledge of the chemical structure of cellulose and later the possibility of reconstituting macro-molecules from oil, allowed the manufacture of artificial and synthetic fibres for which the path from primary material to finished product depends essentially on what one calls scientific knowledge.

The period between 1750 and today has thus been marked by two technological waves. The first wave arose at the end of the eighteenth century and it is characterised by the implementation of traditional innovations in a favourable economic and social environment, that of Europe of the century of light, and more particularly that of British liberalism. It was a major quantitative step, a take off in the sense of Rostow.

The second wave was in the middle of the nineteenth century. It is characterised by a close union between science and technology, which allowed the latter to give to economic activity a qualitatively different push from that given at the time of the industrial revolution of the eighteenth century. The innovations which appeared from then on (at least the essential innovations) are no longer due merely to common sense, experience, and tenacity; they are also the product of the application of fundamental scientific knowledge, applied to the resolution of concrete industrial problems.

Up to a point, the second technological wave is due to the first. In fact on the one hand, the general economic development in the Europe of the nineteenth century allowed the greatest diffusion of scientific knowledge; on the other hand, industrial progress has made available to researchers a large number of measuring instruments without which the breakthrough in experimental science could not have occurred.

One must, however, take cognisance of the fact that these technological waves only gradually made their effect felt in the economic domain. While technical progress is a necessary condition for rapid development, it is not a sufficient condition. The social structure must be sufficiently mature and sufficiently favourable to the introduction of new technologies for these technologies to be able to have a real economic impact.

So the technological progress in Great Britain in the eighteenth century waited until the years 1820 to 1830 to be echoed in the economic structure of the continental countries. For certain countries, particularly Germany, it was necessary that a certain number of political conditions be fulfilled before innovations could be really introduced. Likewise, the effects of the technological revolution at the end of the nineteenth century only gradually emerged, dependent on the more or less favourable social and political conditions. After a first wave of innovations around 1880 (see Fig. 1), there was a technological slack until 1930. The introduction of new technologies was accompanied by severe upheavals which shook faith in progress: the lowering of prices, falling profits, social tensions, the resurgence of protectionism and the formation of cartels were some of the phenomena which did not encourage innovation and entrepreneurs taking risks. It was necessary to await the eve of the Second World War, with economic policies oriented to an increase in demand, for a resurgence of new technologies. The full utilisation of all scientific knowledge of potential interest for industry only occurred after the Second World War. That is why one can say today that the great period of economic growth of the years 1945–1970, exceptional for their intensity and duration, has its roots in the technological changes in the period 1860–1870.

It is not necessary to dwell here on the considerable beneficial effects of these two technological waves. In brief, these effects have emerged in the form of a remarkable elasticity of global supply of goods. Stimulated by the development of productivity, supply has frequently been in a position to exceed effective demand, which has led, all through the nineteenth century and until 1930, to the appearances of crises of overproduction and by a tendency for prices to decrease which has already been noted in the last chapter.

At the level of economic policy, this has led to Keynesianism. In a situation in which supply seemed subject to no constraint, it was natural to concentrate attention on the obstacles to the appearance of sufficient

Long-Term Economic Movements

effective demand and on the resulting disequilibria. Keynesian theory, turning on the role of demand as a motor in the economic process constituted the historic (and belated) response to these problems. The prescriptions of economic policy to which this theory led to stimulation of demand by whatever means, including borrowing and inflation, could contribute to bringing the economy out of the difficulties which in fact reflected a specific historical situation.

Altogether the statistical observations concerning long-term economic movements can be interpreted as follows. The industrial revolution of the eighteenth century and its diffusion on the continent allowed the appearance of a first great wave of economic development. The marriage between science and technology at the end of the nineteenth century created conditions for the pursuit and accentuation of this development. But the potential for increase of the global supply was such that western society at the end of the nineteenth century could not entirely absorb this new technological shock. It was necessary to wait for the middle of the twentieth century, with new more progressive political structures, and the emergence of a new economic philosophy (Keynesianism) for potential supply to be able to find effective demand for the second technological wave to come to fruition.

Relating this to the actual situation at the beginning of the 1980s, the salient question is this: will the second technological wave still have an impact on economic development? In other words, can one attribute the contemporary economic problems to the depletion of the innovatory potential created by the marriage between science and technology at the end of the nineteenth century?

The following paragraphs are devoted to an examination of this point.

3. The Hypothesis of a Slowing Down of Technical Progress

The essential role of technology is to allow increased production with the same or lower input of factors of production. Technical progress thus allows us to combat the tendency to decreasing returns to factors of production.

Fundamentally, the industrial revolution was a period during which technical progress, under favourable cultural, social and political conditions, allowed the reversal of the trend to decreasing returns.

> Global supply and especially the supply of industrial products, has thus shown remarkable elasticity.

But this phenomenon was not immediately noticed by the thinkers of the time. The classical economists (Ricardo, Malthus, J.S. Mill) remained rather sceptical about the possibilities of technology. The economists of the second half of the nineteenth century, especially Marx, were more aware of the importance of the phenomenon, and also of the fact that they lived in an era which was particularly important on the technological level, that of technological progress based on scientific knowledge. Overall, however, and until the twentieth century, technological potential was underestimated. Even the entrepreneurs, collectively, suffered from a cultural delay in this area. It took several decades for them to realise that scientific research could be a source of profit for them. Those who understood this, particularly in chemistry, were able to set up the bases of durable industrial power.

In fact, the first important research and development laboratories were started in the United States, in the 1930s, both within and outside companies. These laboratories were set up to engage in fundamental applied research so that the potential for technological development could be systematically applied to profit.

The Second World War then gave a considerable push to these developments, so that the western world found itself at the end of the 1940s with a professional and efficient apparatus of research and innovation.

From that moment, it became evident that economic growth is linked in an essential way to the potential for technological innovation. The cultural lag had disappeared. One realised (see Schumpeter) that the innovative process was the source of development, not only because it allows the lowering of production costs, but also because it gives rise to new industrial sectors which stimulate investment.

However, one can imagine that this realisation and the resulting full exploitation of technological potential have pushed the system to its limits. This hypothesis, analysed in detail elsewhere (see Giarini and Loubergé, 1978), rests on three main arguments:

First, the professionalisation of fundamental and applied research has decreased the stock of scientific knowledge immediately available for innovation. Technical progress is thus directly subject to the constraint of there being available scientific discoveries. It is no longer possible to benefit, as was the case in the middle of the twentieth century, from the effect of a cultural delay.

Now scientific progress is today confronted by enormous difficulties. And it is further subject to the laws of chance. In physics, for example, progress today depends on the discovery of links uniting the different forces of matter in the macroscopic and microscopic universes. It is necessary to integrate the four forces: the weak force, the strong force, the electromagnetic force and the gravitational force. But there is uncertainty as to the time necessary to obtain a homogeneous theory, and even on the possibility of arriving at one.

Further, the problems of delay also appear at the level of technological development. The application of innovations requires more and more time because the techniques used are more and more complex. The rocket Saturn 5 and the spaceship have, for example, been constructed after a delay of 10 years. And even at the level of simpler technology (see the examples given in Giarini and Loubergé, 1978), one sees that often one or several decades are required to proceed from the first prototype to commercial utilisation on a large scale.

These thoughts cast doubts on the reality of contemporary technological potential. If this hypothesis were true — and we shall consider it again in the third chapter — it would then be possible to attribute the present economic difficulties to a lack of fundamental innovations or to the difficulty of putting them into effect. The present situation could be compared with that of the middle of the nineteenth century, when the first technological wave started to diminish (see Landes, 1972, p. 211), and when the second had not yet made itself felt.

However, there is another possibility. The success of modern technology over the course of the past decades is not independent of the economic structure in which this technology has been applied. In a world which is in the process of industrialisation, the introduction of a science-based technology was equivalent to the application of a new factor of production which allowed an increase in efficiency of the productive process. Technology then gave increasing returns. Now this technology has also had the effect of changing the economic and social structure. The salient question is then the following: in contemporary economic and social conditions, is the technology of the second wave still as productive? Will an increase in technical progress still guarantee an increase in economic growth as was the case in the past? In other words will technology based on science still give increasing returns?

The following section attempts to give some replies to these questions.

4. Decreasing Returns to Technology

With the joint effects of the increases in concentration and in specialisation, the industrial system has become more and more complex. The situation is now depicted in Table 3, rather than in Table 2.

At each stage of production, from raw materials to finished product, the activity of organisation, inventory holding, maintenance, repairs, coordination and in general of information, have increased to such a point that today they constitute a large part of the costs which determine the final

TABLE 2. *The process of industrialisation and value of production*

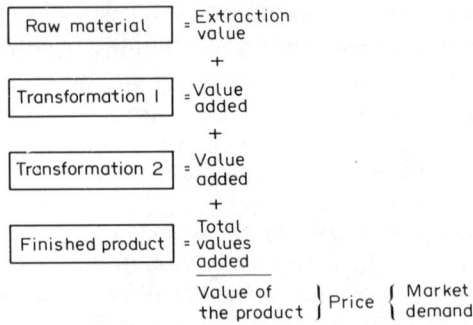

TABLE 3. *Waste and the production process*

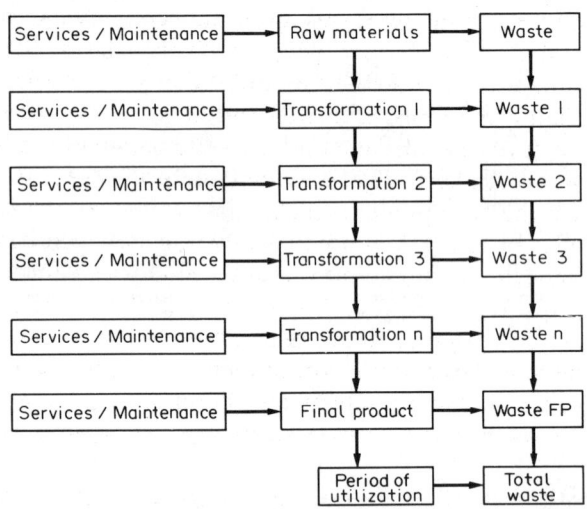

price of products which we buy. If one examines the cost of production of any product whatever, taking account only of what was considered at the beginning of the industrial revolution as being the pure and simple production process, one finds that this often does not exceed 30% of total costs, and that, very often, the percentage is less than 20% and even sometimes close to 10%.

Besides, there is the increasing need to take account of the costs arising during and after use of the products. These implicit costs of maintenance, of use and of re-cycling are added to the cost of production to give the social cost of use of the product.

One should note that the increase in cost of every sort of service is not something which has just developed outside, but also within the productive system. Thus the "vertical" subdivision between the primary sector (agriculture), the secondary sector (industrial), and the tertiary sector (services) is increasingly incorrect. The notion of post-industrial society does not refer to an increase in the tertiary sector but to a "horizontalisation" of functions through the three sectors. On the one hand the industrial sector is becoming increasingly "tertiarised", and on the other hand the primary and tertiary sectors have seen more and more industrialisation of their operations by the application of tools and machines (see Giarini, 1980, pp. 111–140).

Thus traditional innovations, those to do with the improvement of the production process, only apply to a subset of the economy which is becoming ever smaller. Even if they are effective on a technical level, their economic return can in the final analysis be very small. Gains of 20% at one stage of manufacturing a product, which represents only 20% of the total cost, are compensated for by an increase in distributional costs of only 5%. Considerations of this type several years ago caused the chemical industry to depart from its strategy of capacity production of ethylene, ammonia and other intermediary products.

In short the successes of industrial technology have generated their own limits by diminishing the quantitative importance of the industrial production process in the strict sense of this phrase.

The decreasing returns of modern technology are further shown by the effects of its application on a large scale. One thinks before anything else of the problems of pollution, due to the fact that science-based technology modifies the structure of raw materials and also alters the natural processes of recycling waste. But one should also mention the problems of vulnerability engendered by the sophistication of the techniques used and by the organisation of the specialised and interdependent systems and subsystems: when all is going well the system performs very well, but it requires little to go wrong to clog it completely. Under these conditions, the application of new technologies can be diverted or abandoned, not because the new technologies are not efficacious, but because they are accompanied by undesirable changes at several levels: technical, social, economic and ecological.

At a still more fundamental level, one sees that the industrial revolution has allowed considerable development of that part of human activity which belongs to the monetarised sector. One must regard this as the natural result of a tendency to specialisation and of capital needs associated with industrial concentration (the two phenomena are in any case complementary).

Now it is clear that well being depends only partly on monetarised activities, those which involve consumption of goods and services. It is also a function of a certain number of activities and situations which can be categorised as non-monetarised exchanges, which form the indispensable complement (the outworkings of cultural and natural wealth, unpaid work, social and family ties, etc.). As long as the extension of the monetarised sector has not really jeopardised the contribution of the non-monetarised sector to well being, all is for the best. Problems have begun to appear when the monetarised sector has reached such a size that the pursuit of its extension no longer produces advantages which compensate for the corresponding decrease in the non-monetarised sector (see Loubergé, 1982).

More specifically, the limits of monetarisation appear in two cases:

(i) When the passage from a non-monetarised activity to a monetarised activity does not represent a real increase in well-being (e.g. the choice which we very often implicitly make between doing something ourselves, and getting others to do it for a price).

(ii) When monetarisation represents costs which have been provided to restore the usage of free goods (for example, sea water for swimming) which have been damaged due to the development of the monetarised sector. It is obvious that in this case the increase in monetarised activity serves only to repair a loss of non-monetarised real wealth. There is no longer creation of wealth, but reparation of the damage caused by the monetarised system.

This problem shows that one of the important tasks for a fair evaluation of the possibilities of wealth creation in the contemporary economy is in the search for a reasonable equilibrium between monetarised and non-monetarised activities. From the point of view of technology this means that the manner in which this has traditionally been used since the beginning of the industrial revolution is perhaps no longer well suited to the objective of real growth and increasing well-being. This is certainly a source of decreasing returns from technology and should not be forgotten when it comes to evaluating the role which technical progress can still play as a motor of economic development.

CHAPTER 3

The Dynamics of Technical Progress in the Contemporary Economy

The preceding ideas have brought out the historic patterns which technical progress imposes upon the pattern of development in industrialised countries. These ideas have led to the formulation of two hypotheses relating to the technological situation in the contemporary world:

— In the first hypothesis the marriage between science and technology is today no longer as productive as it was yesterday. The problem is on the quantitative level: there is a lack of basic innovations, due to a shortage of fundamental inventions.
— In the second hypothesis the marriage between science and technology is no longer as productive on the qualitative level: the innovations which are still able to be produced are no longer the source of as much economic development, either at the level of the firm or at the level of the whole economy.

Starting from these two hypotheses, the present chapter is arranged in three sections. In the first section, we try to verify the two hypotheses above, by considering the evidence given by practitioners of research and industry. In the second section we try to synthesise the role of technology in long-term movements, allowing for the points of the first two chapters and the evidence of Section I below. Finally in the third section we propose some broad principles for economic policy of research and development which would take account of the lessons from the present report.

1. The Results of a Preliminary Study

The two hypotheses of slowing down of technical progress and of decreasing returns from technology have to do with the long-term wave actually in progress. It is impossible therefore to verify them statistically, if only because of the delay between invention and innovation. One cannot know today which are the contemporary inventions which will lead tomorrow to basic innovations, nor can we assess with any certainty the economic impact which the innovations actually in progress will have in the next 10 years.

Conscious of this constraint, we have chosen to proceed via a survey to verify to what extent theoretical ideas on long-term movements and the technological dynamics of the contemporary world are corroborated by the experience of practical men. The visits/interviews have been carried out with 20 firms and research centres from a wide range of economic activities. A breakdown of the sources of these 20 interviews is given in Table 4.

TABLE 4. *Classification of interviews by sector*

Sector	Industry	Services	Research	Total
Branch				
Textile			2	2
Metallurgy	1			1
Cementeries	1			1
Chemical industry	3		1	4
Food industry	2			2
Automobile	1			1
Engineering		2		2
Electronics and informatics	3	1		4
Energy			2	2
Aerospace	1			1
Total	12	3	5	20

The number of visits made is without any doubt less than the optimal level which one would need to reach in a more ambitious study. Nevertheless, while taking cognisance of the exploratory nature of the present report, it allows us to form a fairly precise idea of the changes in progress today in industrial research and of the reactions to them by the people who have been led to effect these changes.

The general impression arising from those interviews can be summarised in five points.

1. Both at the level of industry and at the level of the centres of research, there exists today great sensitivity to the question of long-term economic movements. Almost all of our interviewees were convinced of the existence of different phases in economic development. They frequently contrast the period 1950–1970 to that into which we have entered since 1970. As regards the causes of these movements, opinions vary more widely. The idea that the lack of basic innovations is the cause of the present difficulties is quite widespread, but there are alternative, or complementary explanations, in particular: the rise in the cost of energy,

the emergence of the Third World on the industrial scene, changes in the social structure of the developed countries. Only one of our interviewees declared himself a follower of Kondratieff's theory of cycles.

2. In the branches which have historically been the source of industrial development (textiles, metallurgy, heavy chemicals, cement, automobiles), it is clear that the era of important technological bonds is over. The general opinion is that we are scraping the bottom of the barrel of technological progress, and that the problems affecting research in these sectors today cannot be surmounted in the foreseeable future unless substantial breakthroughs occur in scientific knowledge. With some exceptions (for example ceramic techniques), the prevailing objective is that of survival. This is further envisaged, symptomatically, in the framework of diversification of activities. For example, in an important professional research centre, the researchers no longer attempt to define the technical–economic area in which their client should concentrate his activities. They would rather try to determine a portfolio of activities capable of generating a regular profit.

Consequently it is obvious that fundamental innovations are lacking in the branches which have until now stimulated economic growth.

3. The decrease in global efficiency of technology is confusingly felt through problems such as the increase in indirect costs of technical progress, the growth of vulnerability, and the distrust by the public of modern technology. Nevertheless, the general impression is that the development of micro-electronics is going to bring important changes at this level. The cost of tertiary activities will be considerably lowered, the systems of production will operate with greater precision and at lower cost, the drawbacks of centralisation will disappear as activities are decentralised.

This gives prospects of real technological development for three essential reasons:

> the costs of production, of maintenance, of upkeep and of administration simultaneously drop thanks to the application of tertiary information and the industrial robot
> the electronic information branch can provide the new demand for investment goods and for durable consumption goods
> this type of development is good in as much as it allows one to overcome a large number of problems with which the traditional type of technological development is faced: tertiarisation of the economy, centralisation of production and of decision taking. Besides, to the extent that the dissemination of information is facilitated, there is the creation of public good, and thus of non-monetarised value.

4. The recent developments of the fundamental research in biology have

created a stock of scientific knowledge as yet unexploited at the economic level. This knowledge opens the door to a new sector of research and development: biotechnology. It is still too early to predict what the real economic importance of this sector will be because the period, now in progress, of applied research and development will last at least 20 years. But two things are sure:

— We are faced with a major qualitative change: the second technological wave was based on scientific progress in the sciences of physics and chemistry; biotechnology signals the entry of life sciences into the industrial sphere.
— Very powerful firms having large financial means have noticed the economic potential of biotechnology, particularly in the areas of agro-alimentation and light chemicals (pharmacy, perfumes, repairing the damage from pollution, etc.). They are heavily involved in this sector because they wish to get in on the ground on something which may be profitable tomorrow. On this point one of our interviewees distinguishes three broad types of industrial strategy:

(i) certain firms will evolve towards biotechnology as the natural extension of their activity (food and chemical industries);
(ii) others will choose an area of bio-industry as an investment; in a strategy of diversification of their activities;
(iii) yet others, finally, with very extensive financial means, will invest massively in the whole gamut of activities of biotechnological research.

One should still note that biotechnology is for these firms a sort of speculative investment. One does not know yet what the return will be. But the simple fact that they are engaged in this area has consequences for contemporary reality, not only in terms of investment, but also because it has certain implications for the future.

5. Two other areas of technological development have been mentioned by some of our interviewees; these are nuclear fusion and solar energy. However the almost universal opinion is that possible progress in these two areas is still very hypothetical. Several decades would be necessary before a real contribution from these areas would be possible.

These results are very valuable in the consideration of the problems which form the subject matter of this report. In fact, and to the extent that they accurately reflect the underlying reality, they partly confirm certain of the ideas which have been presented in the first two chapters. But they also focus attention on developments in progress. We should now examine to what extent these developments can find a place in a general thesis of long-term technological movements. In other words, we should now try to synthesise the different theories and observations which have been presented up till now.

2. Technology and Long-term Economic Movements: Attempt at Synthesis

All the authors who have dealt with long-term economic development agree that the two centuries following the industrial revolution of the eighteenth century have been marked by different periods, alternating between a slowing down and an acceleration of economic growth. Some of them have sought to discover regularities in the alternation of these periods (Kondratieff's cycles hypothesis), but their attempts are not really convincing. It seems that there is in fact no mechanical law of economic movement which is responsible for the appearance of these different periods. More precisely the economic mechanisms certainly play an important role in the dynamics of each period, but they cannot by themselves explain the succession of one period by another. To do this, one must take account of the interactions between economic logic and the historical evolution of the scientific, political and social structure. When one thinks about the long term, it is impossible to consider the economic process in isolation from its environment because this is not fixed.

All the authors have linked long-term economic movements and technical progress. But the role which they attribute to technology varies from one author to another. Many simply see technology as an endogenous factor, unable to launch long-term movements, but which determines the strength of these movements: upon the occurrence of some trigger, new innovations are put on the market and new industries appear, and this then suffices to guarantee the length of the following wave of four to six decades. Others, we among them, think that technical progress is the main force behind long-term movements. We think that the long-term movements cannot be evaluated relative only to innovations, but to the historical evolution of the entire scientific and technical environment. In this framework, technology is no longer just an endogenous factor. It figures, along with scientific progress, among the exogenous elements, the dynamics of which exercise an influence in the economic sphere.

It is agreed by everyone that in a market economy the flow of innovations depends on the entrepreneurs' anticipations of profit. But one must avoid drawing false conclusions from this correct premise. In fact, it does not mean that innovation depends only on general economic conditions, in which case innovation would be really an endogenous factor. Prospects of profit can only be positive insofar as research and development is mirrored among entrepreneurs by unused technological potential. In other words, the stock of scientific knowledge, its evolution in quantity and quality, exercises a constraint on the dynamics of technical progress, and further constrains the capacity of this latter to encourage long-term economic growth through lower production costs and the appearance of new products stimulating demand.

This fundamental fact has been ignored by most of the authors interested in long-term economic movements, perhaps because they neglected to consider the totality of the scientific and technical processes, or because they were struck by the experience of the last two great economic downturns (end of the nineteenth century and the 1930s). In these periods, it is true, the technological potential was high, and the obstacles to development were especially at different economic, social and political levels. So it was tempting to formulate general theories which made innovation an essentially endogenous factor. Applied to the contemporaneous situation, that of 1980, these theories all attribute economic slumps to the difficulties of free enterprise: for a Marxist like Mandel, these difficulties are due to the tendency for the profit rate to fall; for a non-Marxist of Schumpeterian leanings, such as Mensch, they are due to seeking short-term profits while a long delay is necessary to develop basic innovations; finally, for the liberals (the "supply economists"), they arise from the socialisation of the economy.

Now all of these perspectives are partial because they omit to consider all the lessons of technological history of the last two hundred years. In particular, they neglect to take account of the existence of two substantial and qualitatively different technological waves. The political and social factors certainly play a role, but for a long-term economic movement to take place, it is not sufficient that these factors be favourable; there must also be an existing technological potential.

Thus the industrial revolution of the eighteenth century could happen because the traditional innovations had germinated in a cultural and political environment which was favourable to the economic development of the capitalist type — that of England of the century of light. The resulting movement of continuous economic growth, which represented an absolutely fundamental break with a past in which the economic growth and boom periods were caused by the good or bad harvest, was prolonged until the middle of the nineteenth century because of the stimulus caused by the diffusion of the industrial revolution to the European continent and to the East Coast of the United States.

In the middle of the nineteenth century, the technological potential from innovations of a traditional character had already been practically exhausted. The cultural, social and political conditions were then extremely favourable to innovation and to economical development; liberalism triumphed, but technology no longer followed. All the important innovations which one could make from the available knowledge and with enough ingenuity had already been made. A lack of new innovations inhibited the pursuit of economic development.

Fortunately the industrial revolution, technical progress and prosperity had created the conditions for a new fundamental breakthrough. They had facilitated the explosion of the experimental sciences, such as physics and chemistry, which were the source of a new type of innovation: technical innovations based on fundamental scientific inventions. The marriage between science and technology signified the creation of a considerable potential for economic development, evidenced by the lowering of production costs, by increasing returns, and by the appearance of a varied range of new products.

But faced with such potential, one again found political and social structures that were too traditional: a society of austere rural and bourgeois people, little inclined to spend money; an atomistic market in which there was basically free competition; state structures not geared to working in with the economy, and only slightly prepared to influence it through the pressure of regulation of markets and subsidy — when necessary — of global demand. All this had the result that the substantial capacity of industrial supply remained largely under-used until 1936, that is until the New Deal, until the ideas of Keynes and Schach, and until the Second World War. After a first flowering about 1860–1870, also linked to the discovery of gold mines which stimulated demand by their inflationary effect, economic development faltered under the effect of price decreases brought about by the appearance of fundamental innovations in an environment characterised by free competition and the absence of demand subsidy.*

The new technological potential could be applied in its entirety after the Second World War, due to the application of Keynesian precepts of economic policy (starting with the Marshall Plan) and to the appearance of an urban society which wished to consume. The period 1945–1970, exceptional by reason of the strength of its economic growth, was in fact just catching up on the progress which had been lost since 1880.

With the 1970s, we have entered into a new period which is similar in some respects to the period in the middle of the nineteenth century between the two technological waves, that of the traditional technology, and that of the technology based on scientific progress. As at that time, the brake on the pursuit of development is on the level of innovation. The type of technological development seen since the end of the nineteenth century reaches its limits essentially for three reasons:

The stock of new scientific knowledge on which it would be based has

---

* On all these points, see the authoritative work of Landes (1972). They are analysed in greater depth in Giarini and Loubergé (1978).

been totally used. It would be necessary for fundamental research in physics and chemistry to undergo a new scientific revolution for a new stock to be built up.

Scientific technology has especially been applied in the production of goods. Now from the very efficiency of this technology, the quantitative importance of production has in relative terms dwindled: the economy has been tertiarised.

Finally the extent of economic development has caused indirect costs (harmful side effects, pollution, social destabilisation) which cast doubt on the utility of economic growth and of the underlying technological progress.

These different elements have been analysed in different works (Giarini and Loubergé, 1978; Mensch, 1977; Schumacher, 1978), and they have been widely recognised as decisive factors by the interviewees and by more recent studies (Colombo, 1981; Norman, 1981).

At the beginning of the 1980s, one cannot, however, exclude the possibility of a large new phase of economic development, due to two factors acting in concert.

— The first factor shows that the second technological wave is not yet spent. The tertiarisation of the economy has provided an incentive to apply scientific and technical progress in the service sector, and still more in the tertiary activities incorporated in the industrial sector (management, quality control, maintenance, etc.). This is the meaning of the information revolution which is currently taking place. The development of electronic applications is important, not only because they increase still further the efficiency of the productive processes (with the introduction of the robot), but especially because they reverse the phenomenon of decreasing economic growth in the tertiary sector.

— The second factor is also quite fundamental. It concerns the potential for new technological development provided by the development of the life sciences. The recent progress in biology has allowed the build up of scientific capital, as happened in the past for physics and chemistry in the nineteenth century. It is probable that this capital will not remain unused. New industries are in the process of being built up, which try to translate this stock of knowledge into new innovations leading to a new type of economic development. The process of research and development doubtless takes time. A real beginning at the industrial level is only foreseen in about the year 2000. But the change is there.

This being so it would not do to hide the problems which remain or which could arise. We repeat that real economic development requires at the same time the existence of technological potential on the one hand, and favourable cultural, social and political conditions on the other. Even if the first condition were really fulfilled for the coming years, one can wonder about the role to be played by the second. The development of information and of the robot implies a transformation in the organisation and the values of society: it creates the conditions for broad decentralisation in tertiary activities and a change in the ways of life. One must then think about the possibilities of social innovation which — attempting to take into account the complexity of society and to satisfy the aspirations of people — will permit the new technological development to be really a harbinger of an increase in well-being.

One can ask oneself the same question about biotechnology. Have we sufficiently reliable social structures to guarantee that the breakthrough in the life sciences in the economic sphere will be really used to promote the general well-being? As long as this point is not considered, as long as we have not explicitly allowed for the costs and benefits of the roads on which we are travelling, one runs a strong risk of striking inertia and rejection which one would be wrong to consider as irrational.

It is especially in this regard that a better knowledge of the life cycle of the industrial revolution and the dynamics of technical progress will be indispensable to avoid errors of economic policy.

3. Some Principles of Economic Policy

From the preceding thoughts and their synthesis, one can try to succinctly draw several broad principles of economic policy. Certainly measures of economic policy are by themselves insufficient to solve all of the problems, but they can facilitate the transitions between the different periods through which long-term economic growth passes. Above all we must avoid the errors which make these transitions still more difficult.

The Long Term

The public authorities must continue in the role which they play today in the support of fundamental research, the source of future innovations. They must, however, also take account of the fact that scientific progress is not uniform and that economic development passes through several phases of differing characteristics. Consequently we must avoid favouring fundamental research in those scientific sectors which have been most productive in the past. Future progress will probably depend on the blossoming of other scientific areas.

Deeper studies of the long-term dynamics of technical progress should be undertaken with the aim of verifying the ideas contained in this report and to adjust them in the light of new experience.

The constraints of economic reality cannot be ignored. If one wishes to retain all the advantages of a market economy, and if one wishes to see the development of innovations, one must also accept the fact that the propensity to innovate depends on the concomitant prospects for profit. This implies, if necessary, subsidy of demand, but also the recognition of the role of profit as a stimulus to individual effort, particularly as regards the innovatory effort.

Finally, one must ensure that the economic structure reproduces the real contribution of technology to well-being. Productivity increases must be measured relative to the final result of a whole series of different operations and activities. In the present situation, technology is often faced with problems of decreasing returns in so far as the increase in the social cost of production outweighs the expected benefits. It is therefore necessary to study the application of a wider economic accounting system which would take account not only of the flow of goods and services, but which would also consider the decrease in wealth which has made this flow possible and the increase in vulnerability which accompanies it.

The Short Term

The historic period in which we live today is characterised by a higher supply inelasticity than in the preceding periods of increasing returns to technology during the two waves of the industrial revolution. It follows that the traditional policies of demand management (Keynesianism; monetarism) are totally inappropriate to remedy the present economic and social problems. It is necessary to substitute a supply policy for them.

Such a supply policy does not consist, as one tends to believe on the other side of the Atlantic, only of measures to encourage industrial production. It must have as its objective the search for an equilibrium between the two sectors of wealth creation: the monetarised sector and the non-monetarised sector.

We must undertake research to find the specific economic policy instruments which are appropriate to realise this objective. *A priori*, one can think that fiscal policy would have an important role to play. It would seem desirable to work through indirect fiscality, all the while trying to adapt this to the needs of social justice (see OECD, 1980). Indirect fiscality would particularly allow the encouragement of an increase of the life of products.

It is also necessary as soon as possible to apply structural reforms to allow a smooth transition from a centralised industrial society to a decentralised post-industrial society which relies largely on the use of information and the robot. This would be accompanied by a decrease in employment. This is why the most urgent problem to solve remains the definition of a new position of work relative to other activities. One must avoid establishing a dual society in which a minority of efficient workers find themselves in the middle of a majority of unemployed and inactive people. It seems to us that this snag can best be avoided by the use of general incentives to part-time working and permanent education, rather than compulsory reduction in working time and financial transfers to the unemployed.

Finally it is necessary to take account of the fact that the period 1945–1970 was a completely exceptional historical period on the level of quantitative economic development. It was the result of particular technical and social conditions which will probably not be reproduced in the decades to come. It would be vain to wish to reproduce them at any price. On the other hand, in our society, there certainly exist resources ready to invest in a new type of development. One must take cognisance of this and find the political and economic philosophy which is best able to mobilise these resources.

References

Adelman, I. (1965) Long cycles — fact or artifact?, *American Economic Review*, **55**, 444–463.
Bossier, F. and Hugé, P. (1981) Une vérification empirique de l'existence de cycles longs à partir de données belges, *Cahiers Economiques de Bruxelles*, **90**, 253–267.
Colombo, U. (1981) L'Europe vis-à-vis du défi technologique des années 80, Communication au Colloque Innovation et Société, Paris, November 1981.
Dowling, J.M. and Poulson, B.W. (1974) Long swings in the US economy: A spectral analysis of nineteenth and twentieth century data, *Southern Economic Journal*, **12**, 41–59.
Dupriez, L.H. (1951) *Des Mouvements Economiques Généraux*, Institut de Recherches Economiques et Sociales, Louvain.
Dupriez, L.H. (1959) *Philosophie des Conjonctures Economiques*, Institut de Recherches Economiques et Sociales, Louvain.
Eklund, K. (1980) Long waves in the development of capitalism?, *Kyklos*, **33**, 383–419.
Forrester, J.W. (1977) Growth cycles, *De Economist*, **125**, 525–543.
Forrester, J.W. (1978) Changing economic patterns, paper presented at a Conference in Chicago on April 27, 1978.
Garvy, G. (1943) Kondratieff's theory of long cycles, *Review of Economics and Statistics*, **25**, 203–220.
Giarini, O. (1980) *Dialogue on Wealth and Welfare*, Pergamon Press, Oxford. (Traduction française: Economica, Paris, 1981.)
Giarini, O. and Loubergé, H. (1978) *The Diminishing Returns of Technology*, Pergamon Press, Oxford. (Traduction française: Dunod, Paris, 1979.)
Imbert, G. (1959) *Des Mouvements de Longue Durée Kondratieff*, La Pensée Universitaire, Aix-en-Provence.
Kondratieff, N.D. (1926) Die langen Wellen der Konjunktur, *Archiv für Sozialwissenschaft und Sozialpolitik*, **56**, 573–609.
Kondratieff, N.D. (1935) The long waves in economic life, *Review of Economics and Statistics*, **17**, 105–115.
Kuznets, S.S. (1940) Shumpeter's Business Cycles, *American Economic Review*, **30**, 250–271.
Landes, D.S. (1972) *The Unbound Prometheus*, Cambridge University Press. (Traduction française: Gallimard, Paris, 1979.)
Loubergé, H. (1982) Note sur l'économie politique du patrimoine, *Revue d'Economie Politique*, **3**, 27–38.
McGuire, J.W. (1981) Le déclin de l'Occident: une analyse de modèles de prévision à long terme, *Revue Economique et Sociale*, **39**, 89–101.
Mandel,E. (1980) *Long Waves of Capitalist Development*, Cambridge University Press.
Marchetti, C. (1980) Society as a learning system: Discovery, invention, and innovation cycles revisited, *Technological Forecasting and Social Change*, **18**, 267–282.
Mensch, G. (1977) *Das technologische Patt*, Fischer Taschenbuch Verlag, Frankfurt a.M.
Norman, C. (1981) *The God that Limps — Science and Technology in the Eighties*, Norton and Company, New York.
OECD (1980) *The Impact of Consumption Taxes on Different Income Levels*, Paris.
Samuelson, P.A. (1972) *L'Economique*, A. Colin, Paris.
Schumacher, E.F. (1978) *Small is Beautiful*, Seuil, Paris.
Schumpeter, J.A. (1939) *Business Cycles*, McGraw Hill, New York.
Shuman, J.B. and Rosenau, D. (1972) *The Kondratieff Wave*, Dell Publishing Co., New York.
Solzhenitsyn, A. (1974) *L'Archipel du Goulag*, Seuil, Paris.
Weinstock, U. (1964) *Das Problem der Kondratieff-Zyklen*, Duncker & Humblot, Berlin.

2

The Notion of Economic Value in the Post-Industrial Society: Factors in the Search for New Economic Paradigms*

1. Introduction

In 1776 Adam Smith laid the foundations of a recognised economic science while trying to answer the question "What is the wealth of nations?" In so doing, he began by defining an idea of value which fairly accurately corresponds to the cultural and philosophical development of Europe and also to the development of economic realities, i.e. the new methods of organising the available human and material resources.

Based on the ambition of universal European thinking, this idea of value has been transmitted through economic theory so far as though it were an *invariable*, i.e. a fixed point of reference which is universally valid beyond time and space, that is to say, specific historical and cultural conditions. This, moreover, despite the fact that the theories of value *within* the industrial paradigm have often changed.

This idea of value has made possible a quantification which gives the illusion of precision through the specific definition of the added value in terms of the price at the moment of exchange, and forms the basis of the assessment of national wealth defined by the gross national product. Thus, an Eskimo producing refrigerators would become richer not in relation to his real needs, but in relation to the fact that he would have a suitable production structure. Likewise, equatorial Africa will always be poorer than the northern hemisphere in that there will never be a real need to develop a considerable heating industry and to consume a large number of products to obtain heat. Similarly, the more an area is polluted, the more potentially rich it is because it will have to invest a great deal of money to

---

* See also *Dialogue on Wealth and Welfare*, a report to the Club of Rome, Pergamon Press, Oxford, 1980.

combat the pollution. In every case, the added value is regarded as *separate* from the non-monetarised environment.

These examples show that, in practice, the products which the industrial society provides represent true wealth only to the extent to which they add to an inheritance of non-monetarised wealth, so that the *overall* result is positive.

The specific feature of the industrial revolution has in fact been to concentrate on the increase in wealth characterised by the fact of being monetarised goods as though, *in every case* they represented a *net* increase in real wealth. Actually, the crisis between ecology and economics as we know it today in various forms and in every country in the world represents the crisis of this simplification. It is ever more obvious that investments in the monetarised economy to repair or balance the direct or indirect types of harm produced by the industrial system itself are not a sign of increasing wealth but one of making up for an increase in poverty caused by the production system itself.

There is, of course, no reason to make a general criticism of the industrial revolution which has, overall, for two centuries, helped humanity to make clear progress in several respects which could not be abandoned. The question rather is to recognise that the process of industrialisation itself is today subject to two fundamental structural changes.

The world-wide spread of the process of industrialisation makes it essential to take note of the fact that, more and more, the production factors usually taken into consideration by traditional economics are only a small part of a much more complex system, both cultural and historic, which must be taken into account for the *overall* results to be really positive.

The industrial system, spurred by a technology which has so far given largely positive results, is itself faced with a position where technological efficiency is falling off. This means that, as restricting factors increase (population growth, depletion of raw materials, etc.), technological innovations can no longer, as has almost always been the case during the traditional industrial revolution, provide compensations for or even positively combat this increase in restricting factors.

Traditional, neo-traditional or contemporary economic theory is still based on a reductivistic cultural layout. This reductive action had the advantage of simplifying steps and decisions for action and thus making them more effective. Now, the negative aspects of this simplification often outweigh the positive effects.

The integration of economic factors and especially the production factors into the social, historical and cultural conditions of the world's countries has become a fundamental condition for the drawing up of a development policy which is credible and useful for the people concerned. It implies a concept of economic value which must be defined in every case on the basis of specific conditions: the wealth of nations is no longer just something which can be defined on an immutable and fixed scale once and for all. The very definition of wealth and welfare has more and more become a matter of a choice of objectives which, if we are really to speak of democracy in this post-industrial era, cannot but be differentiated in time and space.

This in no ways means that there is not a large number of important economic activities which must be expressed and even organised uniformly at world level: this is why it is important and urgent, for example, to improve and stabilise international monetarised relations.

It is nevertheless necessary to refrain from putting forward a "Cartesian" rationalistic view, a single development model, through the false claim that it is a more scientific method than any other.* It is necessary, in other words, to hinge solutions and methods on the realities which govern what is known as economic activity. Any claim to a general uniformisation in instruments, measurements and objectives can in reality only aggravate conflicts and render the planet ever more ungovernable. The source of so many crises and even atrocities in the modern world does not lie only in the fact that, by and large man has not yet truly attained real civilisation. Many setbacks are also caused by the fact that the cultural instruments which control economic activities at present oscillate between elegant rationality and abstract demonstration and the irrational way in which they are empirically applied.

It is not the intention with these criticisms to belittle the importance of the economy and certainly not economic science, but to suggest a fundamental and essential updating. It is necessary to return to the fundamental questions which were those of Adam Smith and to make a deep investigation to discover what, in every part of the world and for the world itself, is the wealth of nations today.

This is a matter which is not only technical but also deeply cultural and even philosophical. We must by-pass a decade of recriminations and enter a decade of proposals. Let us therefore resume the discussion where the great crisis of modern economic culture began, from the deep implications of the Club of Rome on "The Limits of Growth".

---

* This discussion is in fact part of a much wider one, that of the meaning of science in the modern world. An introduction to the subject has been given by Edgar Morin in his articles "For Science" published in *Le Monde* on 5, 6, 7 and 8 January 1982.

2. The Limits to Growth Re-examined

The name of the Club of Rome has been closely associated during the past ten years with the fundamental debate on the limits to growth. It was (and is) essentially a debate on "how much is too much" — how much population, how much energy consumption, how much industrialisation, how much pollution, how much consumption of raw materials and products, is too much?

But where is the yardstick to tell whether something is too much? To define the level at which the world can support a sustainable order? Who says what is too much and why?

Geologists say that the amount of raw materials in the earth's crust is enormous. Physicists will confirm that the amount of energy in the universe is infinite, at least in relative human terms. The amount of usable space for the human species both on earth and in at least our galaxy is also probably unmeasurable. But the real point is this: do we know how to gain access to all these raw materials and energy and space; and if so, at what cost?

The answer to the first part of the question is linked to the level of knowledge — both scientific and technological — which is available. The question of the limits to growth becomes then a question of the present limits of our scientific knowledge and of the applicable technologies.

The answer to the second part of the question concerns the economic limits to growth, beyond which no scientific approach and no technology that is available can really add anything more to wealth and welfare. To extract gold from sea-water involves processing costs which are greater than the value of the gold that can be extracted. Such an industrial endeavor would thus be wealth-destructive.

The limits to growth are not absolute limits: they reflect the limits of our knowledge, the limits of science, the limits of technology, the limits of economics when it comes to changing the order of things and increasing our wealth and welfare. These limits can be illustrated by putting very simple and practical questions, such as:

> "How many years will it take science and technology to develop the necessary knowledge to make energy production cheaper and danger free?"

or:

> "How many years will it take for any major resource in the world to become available in much larger quantities at less cost and effort and at an acceptable level of pollution?"

Two centuries of industrial revolution have shown that such questions can be answered satisfactorily, within a comparatively limited period of time.

We do not know how soon, if ever, this and other similar questions will be answered in the "traditional" manner. There are at all events some doubts concerning the idea that we must just wait for a new "traditional" cycle. In any case it should be realised that throughout the period of the industrial revolution and up to the 1960s, the economic potential of available technology was more often than not *underestimated*. This has created the false impression that technology would always follow the stimulation of *other* social and economic factors or mechanisms (thus the idea arose that, "given sufficient investment and profit incentives, technology can do anything!").

The "Limits to Growth" report to the Club of Rome has been resented not merely for its economic implications, but because it seemed in fact to undermine the idealistic faith of the industrialised countries in science and technology. When the majority of economists criticised the Club of Rome for not having taken sufficiently into account the future progress of science and technology, it was simply because these economists equated such progress with abstract human inventiveness instead of regarding it as a factual process subject to its own laws of discovery, development and application within concrete limits of time and space. In other words, the reactions against the first report to Club of Rome have been essentially *ideological*.

But the "crisis" of the industrialised countries since the debate on the limits to growth, and even more since diminishing rates of growth have been experienced, does not constitute an exclusively "economic" problem. If we recall the fact that the average rate of growth during the whole of the industrial revolution has never been more than 2% or 3% per year in terms of GNP (which is the present "crisis" level) we must look for some other explanation for these feelings of crisis. They probably derive from the fact that the verified limits to growth seem to call into question the industrialised nations' idealistic assumption of the infinite capacity of invention. In fact, this is attributable to an error which has been accumulating for a long time and which has distorted attitudes towards science and technology. The limits to growth are thus implicitly connected with the limits of knowledge and of science and technology. Accepting the existence of such limits and making an effort to identify them clearly, is tantamount to setting new goals. The scientific process is a process of discovering ignorance and identifying limits and ways to overcome them. Denying that limits exist, denying ignorance, is all too often a sign of superstition, whereby science is equated with a powerful form of magic. This is why the problem of discovering the limits of science and technology, of their significance, and identifying the "diminishing returns of technology", constitute a cornerstone in the search for new forms of progress.

3. Ecological Economics: The Fallacy of the "Rising Expectations" Theory

It is rather common for economists to hear references to the phenomenon of rising expectations. What is generally meant by this is that economic growth does not seem to satisfy people because the richer they become, the more their needs and expectations increase.

In our view, the theory of rising expectations is an economic fallacy, which shows the limits and shortcomings of the notions of value that underlie most current economic theories. Let us consider a specific case.

In the years of great industrial growth it was clear that a family buying more and better food, a washing machine and a car was adding to its wealth and welfare. All these "added values" are evidence of an increase in wealth and welfare.

But when, in a mature industrial society, the same family must, for instance, dispose of one kilo of waste per person per day, the need is then created to buy a waste disposal unit. If the waste is taken care of by the city services, they must be paid through additional taxes or rates. In all these cases the family has increased its expenditure (the family must earn more money in order to buy the waste disposal unit or pay for the services), but has not added to the real value of its wealth and welfare. Rather, it has "deducted" value: money which could have been spent for additional enjoyment, must be spent to meet the costs induced by the maintenance of the economic system. In fact, when it pays for the disposal of waste, the family is in practice paying the additional hidden costs for utilising the products they dispose of (an empty bottle or box, an old machine, etc.).

It can be observed that the more an industrial system develops, the greater the hidden costs (for maintenance, repair or protection) become. More and more induced needs are then created which do not express any true psychological dissatisfaction of the consumers. There is rather a switch from expenditures which produce a net real increase in wealth and welfare to other expenditures which are essential merely to keep the system going. Thus, the family's capacity to spend and will to buy do not represent an equivalent amount of increase in real wealth. Whatever the family members' expectations, they are more and more frustrated, because the more complex the economic system grows, the more they have to use their money to cope with new problems rather than to add to their pleasure.

Even if we disregard completely the effects of inflation, it is easy, for each of us, to determine how much of the costs of products and services used in an advanced industrial country is absorbed by "bound" services and maintenance and repair costs, as compared to these expenditures which really provide a net increase in wealth and welfare.

If, for example, an anti-pollution program absorbs 2% of the GNP,

The Notion of Economic Value in the Post-Industrial Society 47

although this is normally reckoned as an increase in the standard of living, it in fact represents the cost of the *inconveniences* produced by products and services, which cannot be considered as a *value added*.

The dissatisfaction normally attributed to "rising expectations" thus appears instead to be due to a fundamental economic contradiction: on the one hand, it is generally assumed that the real standard of living rises if the Gross National Product (the sum of all the national added values) grows. On the other hand, it is felt, at least intuitively, that real wealth and welfare very rarely grow in proportion to the growth rate of GNP. Recognising this discrepancy between what is measured by economic theory as value and the real changes in the levels of wealth and welfare should produce rather important changes in the way economic development is defined and targeted.

As a start, value should measure real net wealth and welfare: in the "Dialogue for Wealth and Welfare" the notion of "utilisation value" is proposed. This notion is closely connected with the recognition that the importance of the ecological movement in the world during the past few years derives fundamentally from an "economic" demand not always explicitly defined: that of using in the best possible way the resources of the world, whether they are monetarised (exchanged) or not, in order to improve real wealth and welfare for people. The ambition of ecology is fundamentally an "economic" ambition: to redefine and propose what is "the wealth of nations".

We face an interesting challenge, in trying to integrate these two "eco" sciences: ecology and economics. Ecology can help economics by raising in a broader perspective those fundamental questions which in the past two centuries have given birth to economic science itself. Economics can help ecology to reach more quickly and more readily the point where aspirations to achieve better welfare conditions are translated into practice.

The fundamental challenge is to define properly real wealth and welfare, and to avoid creating poverty by the development of inappropriate "values added".

Zero growth or negative growth in real wealth and welfare are very often present even when the economic indicators of the GNP are positive. Such divergent movement indicates that the industrial revolution is giving birth to a new economic reality. The debate on growth/no growth is then totally distorted, if the concepts of real wealth and welfare and of GNP are confused.

Such a confusion is parallel to another one between "economics" and the "economy". Analysing the realm of application of these two terms, we can tackle the problem of defining the notion of value from another angle.

4. Economics and the Economy

The *economy* defines that part of human *activity* devoted to the production and consumption of wealth and the promotion of welfare. As such, it is concerned with the identification, invention and utilisation of resources that are both material and cultural. Explicity or implicitly, the purpose of such activity includes goals of a general and a particular nature, such as survival and the enjoyment of life in the broadest sense.

Economics is in principle concerned with that set of coherent *theories* aimed at providing a consistent insight into the way the economy behaves. Such consistency is normally proved by the capacity of the theory (or model) to provide useful and usable predictions of such behaviour in global terms (macroeconomics) or in specific and sectorial terms (microeconomics).

It is obvious that economic *activity* runs parallel to human history. The manufacture and use of tools by prehistoric man was already indicative of a capacity to divert labour from the production of consumption goods to capital goods and to develop newer technologies and know-how even in the complete absence of money. Observations and even embryonic *theories* can be found in most ancient literatures. But they are normally diluted within the general description of society.

It is generally accepted that *economics* as a specific discipline or science took definite shape in 1776, when Adam Smith published his book *The Wealth of Nations*. As Alfred Marshall put it, "his chief work was to find in the theory of value a common centre that gave unity to economic science".* This unity was consistent both with historical facts and with the cultural paradigms or principles of the European culture of his time. The main fact was the birth of a great period of economic development known as the *industrial revolution*, based on three major interdependent factors:

(a) The development of the *industrial* mode of production to such an extent that it became, for the first time in history, the *first* and decisive factor in the production of wealth and the basis of power. Contrary to Quesnay, who still described wealth as essentially dependent on agriculture, Adam Smith detected, from his personal empirical observations during a couple of dozen years of the first stages of industrialisation (at that time still a very minute phenomenon), the grounds on which the wealth of nations would be built.

(b) The development of new technologies and the technical means of using them, through a process of concentration (economies of scale) and specialisation.

---

* A. Marshall, *Principles of Economics*, 8th edition, p. 627. Macmillan, 1977.

(c) The monetarisation of the economy to an unprecedented extent. Ivan Illich* has calculated that in the sixteenth and seventeenth centuries in Europe only 1% of the average lifetime of a European person was dedicated to remunerated work. In our time, this percentage would be around 16%. This means that if money has always been used, it is only since the industrial revolution that its quantity and circulation have become of real *general* economic relevance. The monetarisation of the economy is the premise that allows capital formation: the accumulation of means and power *through* money becomes more and more important. This accumulation is the condition that permits the use of more and more concentrated (and expensive) technologies; it is the best solution to an obvious logistic problem, one which made it impossible for the industrial revolution to have started earlier (most of the technologies of the first industrial revolution were almost within reach already before the fall of the Roman Empire).

5. Economics as a Theory of the Industrialisation Process

It is important, in our view, not to underestimate the fact that *economics* itself is a *consequence* of the birth of the industrial revolution. For Adam Smith it is clear that the real productive value which adds to wealth is the one emanating from what we now call industrialisation or the industrial mode of production.

A lot of improductive value is produced, or unproductive labour performed, in society, by activities such as those we now call services or the tertiary sector (doctors, lawyers, financial services, insurance).†

In other words, the *specialisation of economics* is such that it tends in fact to concentrate from the beginning on the industrialisation process. The notion of value itself selects what will or will not enter into the analytical models.

But such selection is not only a matter of personal preferences: if it had been, it might have changed after Adam Smith. On the contrary, with time, this selection has become more and more precise, for much more deep-seated reasons. Some of these stem from the very basis of European philosophy.

In order to found a new discipline "scientifically", it was not sufficient,

---

* I. Illich, Shadow Work. Paper presented at a conference in Kassel, September 1980.

† "The labour of some of the most respectable orders in the society is, like that of the menial servants, unproductive of any value . . . the officers of justice . . . the army . . . protection, security . . . churchmen, lawyers, physicians, men of letters of all kinds . . . buffoons . . . opera singers . . . (A. Smith, *The Wealth of Nations*, pp. 430–443. Penguin Books, 1977 (first published 1776).

and it is still not always sufficient, to provide a verbal definition. To be "scientific" a theory must be verifiable and "facts" have to be *measurable*. It is on this point that Adam Smith provided the definitive foundation of economics: the notion of value *quantified* through the price system. The market system (the "invisible hand"), through the supply and demand law, establishes a price, in order to remunerate the value produced by man. At this point, a series of important comments should be made:

(i) The importance of the "invisible hand" lies primarily in the fact that it suggests the idea that price is an "objective" measurement. This aspect is much more important than the interpretation of the notion of the "invisible hand" as a fundamental plea for economic liberalism. This is only partly true. It is the "objectivity" side of it which really matters and opens the door to the "scientific" pretensions of economics in all "political" directions. It is not really an accident that Marx was to a great extent a follower of Adam Smith (the invisible hand depends for Marx on another "objectivists" concept: the class struggle. The search for objectivity has the *same* philosophical foundation).

(ii) Thanks to the tool provided by quantifiable (priced) values, economists have hoped to become as "scientific" as researchers in the natural sciences, who can largely determine the systems or models they analyse through the measurements of specific factors (heat, speed, weight, inertia, resistance, wave-length, etc.).*

(iii) If priced values are the key to economic analysis, then economics must centre almost exclusively on *monetarised* production and consumption systems. Although traditional economists still write extensively about non-monetarised utility values, they will with time abandon this notion, on the one hand because they work more and more on the assumption that what is "free" is not scarce and therefore place it outside the economists' pale (which in our view is largely wrong), and on the other because they see no way of measuring them properly (because of their implicit Cartesian premises). Other economists have tried to broaden the spectrum of economics by introducing the notion of "shadow" prices to account for some of the now monetarised values: in our view, this procedure is of limited interest because the problem today is not one of fitting the facts of the economy to existing economic theory at any price, but of verifying in depth whether the fundamental question of how to create values that increase the wealth of nations can find consistent answers within a

---

* In point of fact, most economists today still *assume* as given a notion of science that is fundamentally positivist, and do not go beyond Newtonian concepts. *See* Mayer (11): this article is written without any *explicit* reference to what hard science is today in the natural sciences, and physics in particular. *See* by contrast W.A. Weisskopf, The Method is the Ideology: from a Newtonian to a Heisenbergian paradigm in economics. *J. Economic Ideas*, Vol. 13, pp. 868–884, 1979.

theoretical framework constructed for the most part on the basis of facts and cultural or philosophical backgrounds different from those existing today.

(iv) It is indeed obvious that the notion of priced or monetarised values is necessarily linked to the situation of a developing economy where exchanges and production follow the monetarised pattern. As we have already stressed, it was precisely during the birth and development of the industrial revolution that the wide diffusion of the monetarised system took place. But even in the time of Adam Smith, only very limited use was made of money in the economic activities relating to production and consumption compared with its use in these activities today. We should note here the great confusion that usually prevails between the stories written about money (its origin and use) and the question of the *transition* of economic activities from a non-monetarised to a monetarised pattern. A key question today is that of the *equilibrium between* the two systems.*

(v) The reason for the decisive growth of monetarisation during the industrial revolution is closely linked to another fundamental factor: the development of modern technology. The more "modern" the technology, the more costly it is, which means that more "capital" (accumulated money) is required. In order to accumulate money efficiently, the economic system must be increasingly monetarised. During the eighteenth century the "capital requirements" in England were, as Adam Smith said, much higher than ever before in history (up to a maximum 5–6% of sales . . .). This percentage reached 12–15% in the last century and 25% and 30% in our time.

Industrialisation therefore is essentially the history of technological development *and* capital requirements, of specialisation and of monetarisation. A society which is not monetarisation-prone has much greater difficulty in using and benefiting from modern technology, as this has evolved in Europe.

(vi) Adam Smith therefore, centering his attention on development and industrialisation *and* founding his economic analysis on the notion of priced value, hit the focal point of economic history during the two subsequent centuries.

(vii) We can only stress the extent to which all these factors are synergically interrelated and correspond to a Cartesian view of logic (rationalism), which in the historical period of the industrial revolution fits fairly well with actual facts. Wealth and welfare henceforth grow in unprecedented proportions.

The process of economic development has been centred up to recent times on industrialisation: economics itself has become essentially a discipline of

---

* See O. Giarini (*Dialogue on Wealth and Welfare*), chapter 3, Pergamon, 1980.

this process, and *not* of *all* the factors contributing to *material* wealth and welfare. But this *reductionist* view has been effective in any case because the *overall* result in wealth and welfare is impressive. Our hypothesis is that the key reason for this success was the availability for more than two centuries of a long-term cycle of *increasing returns on technology*.*

In this context, it should be noted that the priority given to industrialisation is evident in the way economic (monetarised) activity is still divided, even today into the primary (agricultural), industrial and tertiary sectors. There has always been great difficulty, throughout two centuries of industrial revolution in adapting agriculture to industrial development, for the simple reason that its economic structure, at least in the initial stages of the process, was essentially non-monetarised, and therefore economically undervalued by the new paradigm focusing on monetarised activities.

The tertiary sector includes a quantity of services of which some are "valued" today and others are not (in terms of GNP accounting). In any case this was a "residual" category of little "economic" interest at the beginning of the industrialisation process. Even today, it is interesting to note in the input–output models how the tertiary and in particular the services sectors are still a "residual" part of the model.

One of the key points that it is important to understand when speaking of structural changes in our present economic situation is that the reality of "post-industrial" or "service" economics is not one in which the tertiary sector has evolved (as various statistics often show). The key to the phenomenon *does not* lie in the growth of this latter sector at the expense of the other two. The subdivision is *no longer vertical: it is horizontal*. On the one hand, both agriculture and services use machinery and capital equipment typical of industrialised activities. On the other hand, the industrialised sectors themselves make increasing use of "service-type" functions, which are very often of the kind termed "unproductive" by traditional economists (although they still employ the greater part of the labour force).†

In our view, it is therefore absolutely inadequate and highly misleading to accept, on the one hand, the idea of the importance of the "services sector" in our society and, on the other, to continue classifying the phenomenon with tools which correspond to largely obsolete circumstances.

The reason why old methods are still applied, even if admittedly inconsistent with present economic reality, is that little revision has been

---

* See O. Giarini and H. Loubergé, *The Diminishing Returns of Technology*, Pergamon, 1978.
† See the second chapter in Giarini, *op. cit.*

carried out at the level of the basic notions at the origin of economic analytical methods.*

6. Economic Theory, Services Economy and the Example of Insurance

It is our thesis that the economics developed as a discipline or a science since the time of Adam Smith, is essentially the theory of the industrialisation process in so far as this process represents the essential or even the exclusive contribution by man to the increase in the wealth of nations. From this angle, all phenomena not part of the industrial mode of production proper are secondary, or considered to be so both in practice and in theory. In our view, this remains true even if the history of economic thinking has changed greatly since Adam Smith, and even if it has come to embrace ever wider horizons. Indeed, even when, in many cases, economics has tried to go beyond the industrialisation process proper, it has always considered this to be the *reference* for any other type of activity. Through shadow-price systems, or by analysing the value of services, economics has always tried to bring analysis back to the industrial "paradigm" as its basic reference. In other words, we consider that "economics" today is less and less related to the "economy", i.e. to the way in which wealth and welfare are today *really* produced and made available.

The roots of this situation have to be sought in the inadequate verification of the extent to which present economic theories, derived from more general scientific axioms and philosophical principles, correspond to present epistemological conditions. In our opinion, economic thinking is still very largely related to traditional Cartesian (and Newtonian) concepts of science.

The Cartesian mechanism of thinking, although effective and influential in situations where industrialisation is the top priority and the best tool for organising wealth and welfare, has raised a series of methodological and practical problems. Isolating monetarised economic factors is a method that is today showing more and more weaknesses. In order to clarify this point, consideration will first be given to the way the notion of science is often perceived in economics.

It was customary in the nineteenth century to believe that the Cartesian

---

* It is also our opinion that although the notion of value is no longer production-oriented (as in classical economics) but subjective (demand-oriented), as developed by neo-classical economists, the underlying Cartesian/industrialist assumptions of the general economic model remain virtually unchanged. Worse still, the subjective value theory is making it more and more difficult, in many respects, for economics to be a helpful discipline in defining and organising the factors of production at the present time. What is badly needed today is a new, post-industrial notion of value, on the supply side.

or Newtonian method of scientific research consists first in defining a situation or a problem clearly, identifying and measuring all its constituents, as if the said situation or problem could be *fully determined* (or at least assuming that anything left out had no appreciable influence on the system under observation). In this way, a water molecule can be isolated and studied. In this way, Newton gave a clear view of celestial mechanics. In this way, the economist hoped to provide scientifically framed and determined "models" of reality. In practice, this is often still the simple — even trivial — method used and still conceived in accordance with the underlying assumption that the reality examined is for the most part "objective". This view presupposes simple systems and, as an essential corollary, the divisibility of time and space.

It has been clear in the natural sciences for many decades that even if a multitude of realities exists which we can profitably research in the "Cartesian" way, when we get down to basic issues (such as: What is matter?) and to issues related to "objectivity" (if such a thing exists), we find ourselves in extremely *complex* and even *indeterminate* systems.*

It has been rather surprising to note during recent decades that while "social" scientists of all kinds — economists in particular — have been chasing after an "objective" image of their "science", and have often implied that science would in this way come one day to bear comparison

---

* Indeterminate used in the sense of Heisenberg. The whole controversy, started by Einstein with his "probabilistic" reality, is an important reference for this point.

W. Weisskopf *op. cit.*, states very clearly that "The Newtonian paradigm used in classical and neoclassical economics, interpreted the economy according to the pattern developed in classical physics and mechanics, and in analogy to the planetary system and to a clockwork: a closed, autonomous system, ruled by endogenous, mutually interdependent factors of a highly selective nature, self-regulating and moving toward a determinate, predictable point of equilibrium. The Newtonian paradigm, in line with eighteenth century thinking, represents economic events as a reality independent of the observer. The observing subject is supposed to be detached from the observed object, but he can grasp this object with his reason. An objective reality, subject to natural laws, is comprehensible to and knowable by human reason. The idea of natural law was the intermediate link between subject and object which, despite their mutual independence, united them through 'scientific' understanding. Thus separate subjects, objects, natural law, and reason formed a quaternal unitary configuration. The natural laws were laws of causation, interpreted as *causae efficientes*, not *causae finales*; as moving forces, not aspirations and motivations; not only in non-human nature but also in the realm of human existence. The goal of this pattern of thought was to predict future events and to arrive at determinate solutions in all dimensions of reality. If all variables, all cause-and-effect relations were known, we could understand and predict the events in the universe, in society, and all human action. The basic conviction of most scientists was — and to a large extent still is — that despite temporary ignorance, ineluctable laws determine all events and actions. No place was left for freedom, choice, uncertainty, and mystery. This pattern of thought was used in classical and neoclassical economics as the foundation of equilibrium models; it was supplemented by fictitious assumptions, such as perfect knowledge and perfect forecasting, and through elimination of time and change by the *ceteris paribus* clause. This paradigm, as applied in economics, was connected with a belief in the beneficiality, justice and fairness of the free market and industrial system."

with the "more scientific" nature sciences, the latter have in the meantime partially reversed the picture.*

The consequence of this for economics and social sciences in general is that their validity is essentially restricted to given (historical) situations and that the word "universal" validity (in time and space) does not mean very much.

If what has been said here is only partially acceptable, it none the less follows that it may benefit economics to call some basic assumptions in question, especially the notion of value, on which economics itself is founded, and its historical and cultural determinants with reference to the notions of time and space.†

As for the traditional limitations of the notion of value in space, the idea has already been put forward by us that space assumes the existence of a

---

* To the point where a Nobel prizewinner like Prigogine now sees a possibility for a "new alliance" between human and natural sciences. These are no longer different in kind: they are simply more or less indeterminate. See Giarini, *op. cit.*, and J. Prigogine and I. Stengers, *La Nouvelle Alliance*, Gallimard, Paris, 1979.

As to Weisskopf *op. cit.* he defines the Heisenbergian Paradigm in the following way: "The Heisenberg's principle of uncertainty (or indeterminacy) implies that — in microphysics — influence of the observer on the position and velocity of particles makes it impossible to ascertain both their position and velocity, together. Thus, the bases of precise predictions are destroyed. This leads to a different view of reality: "There is no complete causal determination of the future on the basis of available knowledge of the present. It means that every . . . measurement . . . creates . . . a unique, not fully predictable situation." The conclusion was drawn that "we cannot observe the course of nature without disturbing it". Niels Bohr has stated that "man is at once: an actor and a spectator in the drama of existence", and Max Born compared the situation to a "football game where the act of watching . . . applauding or hissing has an influence . . . on the players and thus on what is watched". Man is a finite and conditioned being. He is conditioned by his anatomy, physiology, life history, social environment, and innumerable other factors. The position of the scientist is not different; he is also a person subject to such conditions: he cannot step outside himself. His cognitive horizon is limited by his conditioning. Within the limits of these conditions man is free, and he can transcend them within limits by his consciousness. However, his knowledge, scientific or otherwise, contains these conditions as (often silent) assumptions. The reality he recognises is true reality under the conditions of his existence. He thinks and knows, but the "he" is a conditioned being.

This ontological analysis contains ideas similar to the indeterminacy principle in physics and could be called the philosophical Heisenbergian paradigm. It is more than an accidental coincidence that in two such disparate fields similar ideas were developed. They are rooted in the spirit of the times. The new ambience in metaphysics, physics, and politics is one of uncertainty. If carried to its ultimate conclusion, the Newtonian model elevates man as the objective, detached, "scientific" observer to the level of an omniscient deity who can foresee the future. In contrast, the Heisenbergian model demotes man to a participant who cannot extricate himself from the reality he wants to analyse. This new world view exposes the helplessness and uncertainty which is inherent in the human situation and which was repressed and denied in Newtonian thought".

It is the recognition that "action is the setting in motion of a new beginning with uncertain outcome", which makes "action" both real and possible.

† More basically it is maintained here that the notion of "value added" has grown more and more insignificant as a yardstick for the measurement of "additions" to wealth and welfare. In some cases, it measures subtractions or deduction from wealth. On the notion of "deducted value". See Giarini, *op. cit.*

structure for the production of wealth and the promotion of welfare that has in point of fact been by-passed by post-industrial society: it is less and less useful to divide the economy into primary, secondary (industrial) and tertiary (services) sectors, and more and more rewarding and "practical" to verify final results achieved by the *integration* of various economic activities.* Furthermore, the interdependence of monetarised and non-monetarised activity should be more adequately appreciated and accounted for. But even more important observations should be made with regard to the notion of time:

> In the Cartesian/Newtonian universe, time is either infinite *or* specific: one can isolate a moment in time. One can statically examine "reality" as if it were a *picture*, freezing all movement. The equilibrium of the universe of Newton is like the equilibrium of the supply/demand curves of the economists: at a *given moment in time* (instant time) the situation is such and such. Simple, definable forces determine equilibrium situations, and each state or situation can be isolated.

Under such conditions, the *relative* behaviour of phenomena in *time* and *space* tends to disappear, or to be represented in a static and inadequate framework.

At this point it has to be recognised that the activity of the insurance industry represents a very interesting situation in which the equilibrium of supply and demand (the price of an insurance policy "today" and the cost of a damage "tomorrow" covered by the policy) is a matter of *real, uncertain* time. Duration of time (how long) and space (the statistical universe) *must* be taken into consideration.

It is easy to appreciate in this case how deep-rooted are the causes that have until now prevented insurance (and services in general) from being considered as important as the industrial activities of production (the latter being more easily reduced to a static framework, although this is also more and more inadequate because of the increasing "lead" times in modern technology). Among other things, Irving Pfeffer has shown that the analysis of risk, particularly of insurance risk, requires a dynamic analysis framework, whereas economic theory has chosen a static method of analysis.†

Thus in economics the notion of value is static (value given at a moment in time, in particular at the moment of exchange). Therefore, in the image of any given model, which in economics seeks to be photographic, several important factors are excluded:

---

* See Giarini, *op. cit.*, the analysis of the post-industrial society, chapters 1 and 2.
† See I. Pfeffer, *Insurance and Economic Theory*, Irwin Horewood, 1956, and I. Pfeffer and D.R. Klock, *Perspectives on Insurance*, Prentice Hall, N.J., 1974.

— not only is the probabilistic evolution of economic behaviour dismissed (as in physics before the 1920s) to the point where the majority of economic models imply the "certainty" assumption (sometimes this is said to be done for the sake of simplification);
— but also any economic behaviour covering any length of time disappears: in the national accounting of insurance, only the employees in the insurance companies are accounted as "added value" (they are paid "now" as in any other sector, which means in practice every month — a short period of time*). The real value of insurance, the increase in wealth brought about by the possibility of controlling future probable damage by means of the insurance system has no "value" . . .

Economists have had to invent a trick to get rid of this contradiction. They speak of "transfers" and the logic is the following: when a house burns down, insurance will pay for its reconstruction (if it was insured). The action of building is real added value and such will appear in future statistics as an increase of industrial activity. Therefore, there should be no need to calculate insurance as value — they say — for it merely organises financial transfers. What is "productive" is the act of building, whereas the act of making that building *possible* is, awkwardly, "non-productive": the old scheme has been saved.

In point of fact, in the case of a house that burns down, what happens in real time and in terms of real wealth is as follows:

— when the house is built it is accounted as an added value, which is only right and proper;
— when it burns down, the level of real wealth is reduced (a deducted value is produced, or a negative added value), but no macro-accounting takes this into consideration;
— when the house is rebuilt thanks to its having been insured, the economic accounting systems register the fact that a new (industrial) added value has been produced. This suggests, by the way, the absurd idea that the greater the amount of fortuitous destruction, the more chances there are of increasing value added. The correction for this is to take into account the deducted value, too;
— the rebuilding of a house thanks to an insurance policy is a value that could be ascribed *totally* to insurance activity. The house might not have been rebuilt without insurance. In this case, the industrial tools are part of the security mechanism (or service) provided *by insurance*.

The traditional economist would say that insurance is paid for its service,

---

* Static time and short time are not the same thing of course, but a "short time" reality allows in practice a "static" analysis, whereas static analysis is useless for long-term phenomena.

which is the organisation of the transfer of money (through the activity of insurance employees and office equipment) and that the money spent on the rebuilding of the house is again an *industrial* activity, producing an *industrial* added value. But this is obviously untrue, at least from the standpoint of the buyer of the insurance, since he buys the possibility of rebuilding the house and not the service of a financial transfer alone. And he buys this possibility from an insurance company, just as the buyer of a chemical plant very often buys the services that go with it, which are not distinguished as non-industrial.

Indeed, the problem is *not* a matter of giving priority today to service industries over industrial producers, but of recognising the integration of the two (and of agriculture) in the production of wealth in a way that is different from the way wealth was produced in the period of the industrial revolution. It could be said that, in practice, the traditional concept of value isolates and gives priority to industrial activity proper, whereas what is proposed here is a new concept of value corresponding to a post-industrial society in order to facilitate the adaptation of the tool of economic thinking to the contemporary economic situation, in which industrial and service activities are at the same level.

When insurance and service activities represented a relatively small part of the economy, this had no great practical effect, especially when the economy was in the upper phase of the industrial revolution. In such a situation, the argument submitted here could be dismissed as intellectual hair-splitting.

The position is different in a post-industrial environment where people at least begin to feel that their wealth and welfare are increasingly dependent on mechanisms that make things possible and accessible, rather than on simple acts of production.* The following example will clarify this point with regard to changes in the economic structure:

After the 1929 slump, many poor people could not obtain food because they lacked money. Food was also destroyed so as not to flood the market and lower prices (thus putting more industries out of business). Keynesianism had its origin in situations of this sort: if people could simply get more money (even by deficit spending) they would buy the existing surplus. Instead of destroying supply it was clearly better to stimulate demand.

At the present time, all governments have learnt — in one way or another — the Keynesian recipes, so that inflation is one of the few certainties of our time (whereas during most of the industrial revolution, *deflation* was the most recurrent phenomenon). But we still have more and more cases of over-production, particularly in agriculture. Farmers quite

---

* At this point, it would be also very useful to open a debate on the notion of stock and flows in the accounting of wealth. See Giarini, *op. cit.*, chapter 3.

often jettison tomatoes, fruit, vegetables, along the highways. Does this mean that people have no money to buy these products? Obviously not.

The problem is not production, but the *cost of access to production*. Such costs are linked to the tertiary sector (services of all sorts), and in every case they are higher than the costs strictly related to production: distribution and service costs command the price equilibrium. Clearly, economic value is related nowadays to a complex system heavily dependent on the ways and means of access to a product (or rather its services): we *are* in a post-industrial society, a *service* society.

If agriculture was the key reference point of Quesnay and of many later economists, if industry has been the key reference point of economic theory up to now, there is reason to believe that in studying the activity of insurance, economists should find an excellent reference point for the definition and rethinking of post-industrial economics. Discussion of the notion of value brought to the fore by risk and insurance-related institutions might be a tool for thorough and interesting research on what, today, adds to economic wealth and welfare and how economic strategies can be improved.

Enlarging on the implicit and exclusive paradigm of economic theory, still predominantly connected, as it were, to the industrialisation process, may contribute towards a more positive view of what future wealth and welfare could be.

7. The Problem of Defining Welfare*

We have tried to highlight, in the previous paragraphs, the fact that the technological revolution, industrialisation and the spread of monetarisation (as the basis for capitalisation in the form of private and/or public capitalism) are all facets of the same phenomenon. They are the reactive elements of a single system — the Industrial Revolution. This has permitted unprecedented growth in human material welfare, being at the same time deeply embedded in a specific historical and cultural setting.

We have also underlined how economics, as an important, new social science (discipline), is largely an outcome of the same industrial revolution. Economics provides light for the analysis of social phenomena, in as much as they become "visible" and quantifiable by the price system.

But the fact remains that wealth, welfare, and well-being are all human aspirations which are not satisfied by priced products alone, *even if they are strictly material*. Furthermore, there are probably many aspects of welfare and of human needs which are a mixture of material and of "spiritual" nature, something like the psychosomatic diseases where there is no

---

* Paragraphs 7 to 9 are extracted from *Dialogue on Wealth and Welfare, op. cit.*.

boundary between the imagination of mental attitude on the one hand and the physical body's reaction on the other. Even further, many would also add that numerous needs are purely spiritual. Monastic contemplation can also be a definition of well-being which is — at least in principle — completely excluded from a monetarised organisation of society.

The notion of welfare (and of wealth, well-being, human needs, etc.), in its widest definition, allows infinite variations. It is something like the wavelength spectrum. The visible light can be compared to visible welfare, expressed in monetary terms. The infrared and ultraviolet waves are not as visible as the light waves, but still relatively easy to detect (particularly infrared radiation which we feel when it transports heat): we could pursue the analogy by saying that these waves might correspond to all those elements of *material* welfare, which are *external* to the priced or monetarised economic system. Furthermore, the short and long radio-waves become more and more imperceptible to our direct senses, but are still essential as carriers of sound: in the economy, we enter here a zone where connotations of material and spiritual well-being are more and more difficult to distinguish from each other.

Finally, since we do not know where the wavelength spectrum starts or finishes at either end, we are here in presence of a *boundary of knowledge* or even of the possibility of inquiry, which probably corresponds to the impossibility of setting any final boundary to reality.

The subdivision of the different types of wavelength and of the different types of welfare and needs, must be understood as a tool for better understanding the problems, and *not* as a representation of reality: otherwise we would fall into the trap of "Cartesianism". In fact, the passage from one type of wave to another and from one type of welfare to another, is a continuum.

In its article on wavelengths, the *Encyclopaedia Britannica* notes that:

> "The various frequency ranges bear different names because of the different behaviour in the emission, transmission and absorption of the corresponding waves, *but they overlap* . . . and . . . there are no precise wavelengths accepted as boundaries between any of these continuous ranges."

Even here, we are therefore not quite in the "Cartesian" system of objectively distinct and separate frameworks.

So much more in the case of welfare and needs, where the subjective elements (the cultural and individual attitudes and conditions) make even more complex the relations between material and non-material welfare, between the monetary and non-monetary.

This subdivision is necessary purely to improve the degree of *approximation* of our analysis. It is not for the purpose of acquiring true knowledge — rather just a little more knowledge (if possible). Experience with "Cartesianism" and everything that followed, as has been outlined in our previous paragraphs, should warn us of the danger of proposing new views which, when they are made philosophically absolute, run the danger of transforming the element of knowledge into an instrument of modern-day superstition.

It must therefore be emphasised that when we propose here apparently clear-cut boundary conditions, they are a tool for a first-step analysis, but they are also an avowal of inadequacy linked to our mind's inability to capture a multitude of elements which exist simultaneously in reality, but which we cannot encompass due to our basic limitations. To understand this better, we just have to look in front of us for a moment: it is impossible to scan all the objects, shapes, colours and movements simultaneously. The eye will detect only a fraction of reality. Reconstruction of this simultaneity of a complex picture is possible only with patient, *ex post*, detailed analysis and synthesis, owing to the inadequacy of our sensorial and mental capacities.

Let us return to our wavelength and/or welfare spectrum having now realised its inadequacies and limitations not just as a "*formule de convenance*" but in a more basic sense. Since total, human and spiritual welfare and needs comprise an infinite range of possibilities, the traditional industrial economic system is the one which is motivated by the effort to increase *total welfare*, through the expansion of the social system which is organised around monetarised forms of relationship.

History has known periods of spiritual upheaval in which attempts were made to increase man's well-being by giving a priority to spiritual goals.

One specific period in human history, the Industrial Revolution, has — thanks to the combination of culture, technology, industrialisation and monetarisation — had the historic possibility of reinforcing in an unprecedented way one part of the human welfare or needs equation.

The most important problem confronting the modern economy here, is to verify how far its *contribution* to total welfare, and in particular *to total material welfare* is still determinant, or at least important.

In the context of Fig. 6, the task is to examine how far economics,

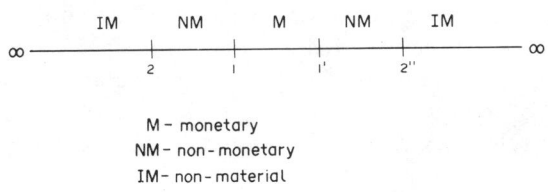

M – monetary
NM – non-monetary
IM – non-material

FIGURE 6.

concentrated in space 1 to 1' (the monetarised zone of the economy) is now being more affected than in the past by the inter-relationship with the wider spectrum of *material* forms of activity producing the welfare comprised between 2 and 2'.

8. Monetary and Non-monetary Economic Values

Human (and even animal) societies have always been faced with "economic" problems: whenever there is scarcity and wherever action is taken to combat it, there is an economic activity, whatever its nature.

The Industrial Revolution has provided the human race with efficient new tools to combat shortages. Industrialisation has become the priority so that even if economics is essentially the outcome of this phenomenon, it will still be sufficient for analysing and for directing policy in the organisation of welfare. It will provide added "production" value, which is supposed to add to the material welfare of any other non-monetarised type of activity, *but this applies under specific historic conditions*.

More than that, substitution of a non-monetary activity by a monetarised activity, even though entailing certain specific sacrifices, will finally be considered desirable: the productivity of the monetarised sector will more than compensate, in the long term, and often also in the short term, for any loss in the traditional, essentially non-monetarised sector. This has been the obvious outcome of the Industrial Revolution.

In other words, if it is admitted that economic, material welfare may also be produced by the traditional, non-monetarised sector, total material welfare (TW) can be defined in general as:

$$TW = V_{NM} + V_M$$

(V — value; NM — non-monetarised; M — monetarised)

A relatively high degree of non-monetarised values has persisted even in the most industrialised nations, e.g. non-remunerated work (housewives, benevolent activities), non-remunerated goods and services (unpolluted air and water). The *historic* evolution of monetarised and non-monetarised economics will be studied in greater detail in the next chapter.

What should be emphasised here is that insofar as V_M is the really dynamic part of the question in adding to TW (where V_{NM} is particularly static and/or irrelevant), then the economist can and does normally assume that $TW = V_M$.

However, V_{NM} is *not* independent of V_M; V_M in fact reduces the field of the NM economy and/or transforms it.

The Notion of Economic Value in the Post-Industrial Society 63

As stated, it is normally assumed that any loss in the *NM* sector will be more than offset by the *M*-substitutive activity. In terms of value, gain in V_M will be greater than any loss in V_{NM}.

But it is only under such conditions that *TW* will, in fact, increase. The difficulty of analysing such an equation is due not only to the problem implicit in evaluating non-monetary activities, but also to the concept of value in traditional economic theory, when this is equated with welfare. We have examined this problem above; we would like, then, here to stress the importance of the non-monetarised part of the economy.

If the notion of value is limited to the monetarised production process, we discover that, in fact, it implies that *any* production, which considers only price boundaries, is producing welfare. This can happen — as we have seen — when the advantages of industrialisation are overwhelming, indisputable and do not suffer from diminishing returns of technology. If the notion of value is based, as we proposed, on its utilisation, it becomes a matter of common sense to identify welfare with the total net contribution of the non-monetarised *and* the monetarised economic system to the satisfaction of material needs.

In other words, the basic paradigm — the concept of value — of traditional economics (be it the Smithian concept, or the demand-based one), represents an obstacle to assessing the true net contribution to welfare by non-monetarised economic activity.*

The following remarks may clarify this:

— A closer look at any production process reveals that, among the production factors, there are many inputs which are not monetary or not monetarised: the cost of the air for a company producing nitrogen through the liquefied air process, is nil, as are the large quantities of river water used by a paper or an aluminium mill.
— If this air or water is highly polluted, costs will be incurred in returning these "free" raw materials to their initial purity — the problem is intensified in that most advanced technology may not be able to avoid pollution emission, and may even tend to aggravate the total environmental control problem.

Consequently, in the initial industrialisation phase, the industrial system will have many essential production inputs "free of charge". Subsequently, they will have to be paid for: this transfer into the monetarised system does

---

* The literature discussing the shift in the economic paradigm is multiplying rapidly. See among others: Henderson, Hazel: Economics: a paradigm shift is in progress, *Solar Age*, August 1978, pp. 18–21; Katscher, Ernst: *Wiedergeburt der Oekonomie*, Eisenstadt, Austria, 1979; Huber, Joseph: *Technokratie oder Menschlichkeit*, Berlin 1979; Siebker, Manfred: Die unsichtbare Hand sichtbar machen, *Frankfurter Hefte*, April 1979, pp. 21–26.

not indicate that a process is increasing total welfare, but simply that it is first of all increasing the total *costs* for producing welfare.*

The same examples can be drawn at the level of the individual: swimming in a non-polluted sea or lake for free is an element of welfare. Invention of the car led to an increase in total welfare by adding to the choice of places to go swimming. There is an obvious increase in total welfare (based on services available from the non-monetarised economy and from the monetarised one). In a third phase, the same industrial system which makes possible the production of cars leads to the pollution of seas and lakes. Thus, there is diminishing welfare (utilisation value): costs entailed in re-establishing utilisation value of the water, will be "catching-up" costs and not costs adding to total welfare (or utilisation value). We encounter here, once again, the concept of value deducted.†

Starting from the *traditional* notion of value, it can be said that, in current economic accounting, a certain number of production phases (and a number of products) are not produced in order to increase added value, but in order to restore utilisation values which have been previously destroyed and which now have to be recycled or reintegrated at some cost, in order to permit the economic machine to run. If the rise in national income in recent years is due increasingly to the development of the anti-pollution industry (detection systems, chemical products, incinerators, waste disposal units, etc.), this production is not adding to the initial level of welfare but it is being used more and more to fight the negative effects of industrial expansion. The resultant added value is not a measure of added welfare: it represents the cost of previous consumption which now has to be paid in order to restore utilisation possibilities. It is, in fact, a *deducted* value. The indicator of GNP as a sum of added values is in fact diverging more and more from an indicator of welfare: it is increasingly clear that it is rather only an indicator of cost. If, in the golden era of the industrial revolution, it could also be assumed as an indicator of material/economic welfare, it is because in a period of no real diminishing returns of technology, almost all the production costs become net real wealth. Now, an ever greater part of those costs represents a negative feed-back loop effect on the overall trend of the total *monetarised cost indicator* — the GNP.

---

* The problems of environmental costs and their discussion are stimulating economic thinking. In a study by the European Trade Union Institute (Brussels, 1979) it is proposed to integrate environmental factors in a new "Keynes-plus Economy". The reference to Keynes is understandable as reaction against a resurgence of conservative liberalism in recent years, which tends to lay at the door of union policies most of the rigidities of the present economic situation in the industrialised countries. It is clear that, from our analysis, both neo-liberalism and Keynesians are still largely prisoners of increasingly inadequate traditional economic paradigms.

† A similar notion has been proposed by Fred Hirsch in his book *Social Limits to Growth*, London 1976, where he speaks of "positional goods".

9. The Time Factor in the Notion of Value

The idea of defining net value in a first approximation, as the differential between total gross added value (as normally computed), less the "deducted values", does, of course, present some problems.

The first is that deducted value represents a cost *in the past*, which has not been taken into account: the pollution of today is the result, in most cases, of negative accumulations in the past, which have not been eliminated. The present has been subsidised by the future: instead of preparing a world for the future generations, many costs have been, and are being, simply transferred in time. As mentioned in the previous section, we find here again a limitation of the static notion of time in economics: added value always seems to be net added value, because it represents a specific moment in time. In other words, if the notion of value is *static*, one can safely state that any production or any investment today — including that in pollution — tends to ameliorate the standard of living. The *future* pollution produced by *present* production will appear as a negative element only later. It may therefore continue to destroy future welfare and still give the impression, in the static analysis, that added value is a real thing. This is an obvious, paradoxical case, in which formal logic, within unverified boundary conditions, leads to absurdity.

As a consequence, a real challenge for economic thinking now, is to explore all possible ways of reviewing the basic notions in a real dynamic time dimension.*

---

* Discussion of "deducted value" also necessarily entails a reappraisal of the economic literature on externalities. Here are some major points:
— Internalisation is not, as normally represented, a marginal economic phenomenon. Rather, in our perspective, it is a fundamental mechanism of the modern industrialised economy: it represents the transition of the economic activities from the non-monetarised stage to the monetarised stage. At any given moment in time, this process might seem marginal: but it is its cumulation in time which really creates the fields of action of "industrial" economics. The historical transition process should be better analysed in order also to verify how much of the increase in "monetary" welfare represents simply a transfer from the non-monetarised economy and how much represents a real added value. We would not be surprised, if, when introducing this notion into national accounting the real growth in GNP were diminished by something like 20% to 50% — even before taking into account the "deducted" value.
— There is a second aspect of internalisation (termed by Simon Kuznets the "negative externalities") which is linked to the diminishing returns of technology.
— It is the moment at which the internalisation of an economic activity is carried out not in order to increase total overall productivity (first case) but because the free elements or factors contributing to the monetarised production need to be restored, by investing money (i.e. investing for pollution). This is the case of deducted values (which remain deducted even when they are "internalised").
For a further analysis of externalities see E.J. Mishan *The Costs of Economic Growth*, Harmondsworth, 1969, as well as "The Post-war Literature on Externalities: an Interpretative Essay", *Journal of Economic Literature*, March 1971.

All this leads to a basic concept, i.e. that of the general source of wealth and welfare, which we have termed "Dowry and Patrimony" (D & P). The book "Dialogue on Wealth and Welfare" is devoted essentially to this concept which is the basic reference for identifying not only deducted value but also the source of utilisation value, as an indicator of real wealth.

However, by now it should already be clear how the concept of utilisation value has both a comprehensive time dimension (real-time continuum) and a space dimension (integration of monetary and non-monetary activities).

We can therefore now add to the monetarised sector, the dimension of the non-monetarised economy and consequently be able to make the following statement:

The utilisation value of products or service is built up and guaranteed by a series of monetarised activities (costs), such as:

production costs;
storage and distribution costs;
maintenance costs;
service and repair costs;
financial and insurance costs;
disposal costs;

as well as of non-monetarised activities and stock of goods and services, such as:

free-labour activities;
qualitative (cultural) performances of people;
free flow of free goods (water for washing and drinking), derived from the natural and non-monetarised Dowry and Patrimony, *related to their life period.*

This definition of economic value, creates probably as many new problems as it solves old ones. But it has at least a fundamental advantage: it simulates a vision which should be capable of mobilising *all real* productive forces in a society and opens up the field to new initiatives for our future.

3
Notes

The Employment Problem

There are two fundamentally different ways of approaching the employment problem:

(i) To regard ourselves as merely facing a period of adjustment and adaptation of the industrial revolution which is reaching a new state of balance without nevertheless deeply altering its connotations. Here, the employment problem principally takes the form of a problem of investing in order to create enough jobs to absorb the available labour.
(ii) A very different approach is to take the attitude that we are no longer living in an industrial society and that the old mechanisms can no longer provide useful solutions. This means that the rules for production and the distribution of wealth, and those governing the mobilisation of productive forces are subject to a different logic from that of the industrial revolution.

In my report to the Club of Rome entitled "Dialogue on Wealth and Welfare", I tried to show that we are now in a structurally different situation from that which has existed during two centuries of industrial revolution. Employment problems can therefore be solved only through a basic change in the economic viewpoint.

1. Change in the Economic Viewpoint

This statement is becoming more and more widely acknowledged in literature.[1]

In the report on "Wealth and Welfare", I give a composite view of this situation (Table 1.4 on pp. 28–29), concerning the tendency of the non-monetarised economy towards more accentuated forms of monetarisation, as far as the point of balance at which monetarisation should be halted (see Appendix).

---

[1] "Work or activities?", by Robert V. Horn (University of New South Wales, Sydney, Australia), in *Work and Society* by the International Labour Organisation, Geneva, 1981.

If these premises are accepted, the result will be that economic policy measures will have to take a positive stance towards unpaid work and occupations, giving them the time and conditions needed for their development.

For this to be possible or merely partly acceptable, it seems substantially pressing to alter fiscal policies. Without such changes, the existing inertia in fiscal policy will continue to counteract any efforts at mobilising and organising unpaid productive activities. One important feature of fiscal policy will once more have to be that of giving preference to indirect rather than direct taxation. Taxes would, of course, have to be scaled according to the requirements of equity and justice. This problem of taxation is also studied in the report to the Club of Rome[2] (Fiscal Policy and Capital Formation).

2. The Reduction of Paid Working Time

The trade unions' present demands for a reduction in working hours are still being made under the traditional view of economic evolution. Only in a very intuitive way do they quote reasons and principles which go beyond the logic of the traditional industrial revolution. We do not believe that a 5% to 10% reduction in average working hours can provide a proper solution to the present economic problems. It seems wiser to open discussion from a quite different point of view.

Instead of considering that the amount of daily paid work to be provided is from 8–9 hours, it would perhaps be more interesting to consider that it could be brought down to 4–5 hours every day. We therefore propose to look into the interest and feasibility of making the reference unit as small as half a day's work (for paid work).

At first sight, this would have several advantages:

(i) it would allow paid work to be linked to what might be called the guaranteed social minimum;
(ii) it would allow members of families to make a more balanced contribution towards paid *and* unpaid activities.

This would open other, new prospects for accumulating working hours within the same family, and it could be varied according to the conditions imposed by the children, the organisation of the home, etc.

If the daily working units were reduced to half a day, it would make it possible for everyone to accumulate two daily units so that, in most cases,

---
[2] *Op. cit.*

it would be perfectly possible and in order to have a paid activity for the whole of the period at present represented by a full day's work. Moreover, variations on the basis of a minimum of 4 hours per day would make it easier to organise jobs requiring round-the-clock working which, once the paid working week drops below 40 hours over 5 days, become rather difficult to organise. Clearly, a very large number of activities can be performed during a paid working day of 4–5 hours. An accurate survey, sector by sector, should be made.

It is also clear that some activities require a continuous presence which is not limited to eight hours alone, but very often extends to the full 24-hour day. Here, it would be perfectly natural to organise a way of always accumulating two 4-hour compulsory units or, at least, acceptable alternatives.

Again, it is obvious that these proposals would have to be examined sector by sector and activity by activity, taking account of training problems which, in a large number of instances, are limitations which hamper labour mobility. Work based on a daily 4-hour unit could also make better organisation of on-the-job training possible. The unpaid period could be still more easily used for all types of training allowing a better individual acquisition of general culture, and providing greater flexibility and adaptability (here, the university and continuous training should overlap more and more).

All these proposals can become credible or only thoroughly discussed on the basis of the idea that, in the post-industrial society, productive activity must be organised both inside and *outside* the monetarised system. This is a crucial point which, I believe, corresponds to a general orientation of public opinion and, in particular, to all those concerned with ecological problems. At the same time, it is an essential transition point between theoretical considerations and the practical significance thereof. In other words, it is necessary to give a fillip to the concept of the value of work in both the monetarised and non-monetarised sectors, and consequently by-pass the economic reductivism of the conventional industrial revolution.

3. The Useful Life of Products and Services and Employment

One of the essential features of the concept of value in the industrial revolution period is that it is determined by an immediate price at the time the exchange is made. In my report to the Club of Rome, I explain why this system is satisfactory in a true industrial revolution situation characterised by increasing technological efficiency. This means that the useful life of products is not essential in assessing the increase in wealth in so far as a technological innovation through the obsolescence of previous methods, makes it possible to improve production conditions. My key theory is to say that this situation, where technology is becoming increasingly efficient, no longer exists and that we have entered a phase of overall decreasing efficiency (meaning that the increase in restrictive conditions like the increase in the population or the depletion of resources is no longer compensated at a comparable rate by technological progress).

In such a situation, the value of goods and services can no longer be identified at the value at the moment of exchange, all the more so since many of these values are in fact the expression of a deduction and not of an addition to wealth. For example, the added value produced owing to progress in anti-pollution activity does not represent an overall increase in wealth, but rather a lowering in the destructive effect of wealth which was not accounted for at the time it was produced.

It therefore becomes important in the post-industrial society to define the value of the use of goods and services, i.e. what they bring as an addition to welfare and wealth during their useful life, taking into account all the costs which have been entailed (during production, use and recycling or waste treatment). In general, therefore, the idea of an instantaneous economic balance must be replaced by one of an optimum real time by a calculation of the costs/profits which should be made during the period of use (real values) of products and services. This reasoning is valid only in so far as technology, as is the case now in many sectors, no longer has the capacity to result in obsolescence, as in the traditional period of the industrial revolution.

To explain the same ideas in a more down-to-earth manner, it is immediately obvious that, from the time when raw materials and resources become even dearer, it becomes ever more important to use the same materials for as long as possible.

It must also be pointed out that, the shorter the useful life of products, the greater the energy consumption at the manufacturing stage (and afterwards, at the waste-disposal stage). Likewise, the longer the useful life of products, the more labour will be needed to cope with maintenance and repair.

Where greater capital-intensity no longer produces wealth, the use of labour becomes more and more competitive and this can be brought about through a production structure which puts a true value on useful life and balances it over a period of time.[3]

---

[3] See table N. 1.3, page 17, of the report on *Wealth and Welfare, op. cit.*, showing the difference between the use of capital and labour for a car with ten years' useful life and one with a useful life of twenty years.

72 Cycles, Value and Employment

A consideration that, nowadays, fiscal and economic policy favour shorter useful lives of products on premises which have now become false, brings with it the realisation that an employment policy is also largely dependent upon the steps which may be taken to optimise the useful life of products. To this end, it is first necessary to make a detailed empirical examination of all the sectors in which the likelihood of technological obsolescence is least for the next ten to twenty years. This exercise is less difficult than is normally thought and affects fairly well known sectors (the motor industry, chemistry, smelting, etc.).

Stressing the useful life of products also means providing room to mobilise unpaid work. In fact, much maintenance, repair work and restoration can be done on an unpaid basis. This is where this second factor in a new employment policy connects with the previous one.

With regard to social security and, in particular, the problems of old people, the best way of ensuring both personal and psychological security is to continue to be active beyond the age of 60. In view of demographic development in Europe and also considering that about 90% of those over 70 are capable of working, the idea of the working unit of four hours makes it possible to give these people an option or a real chance for security. Clearly, there is no point in including everyone up to the age of 70 or 75 in the labour force unless the basic unit is about four hours a day.

Appendix. Capital Requirements: Labour and Productivity
The Limits of Monetarisation[1]

1. In the *pre-historical World*, men's labour to survive is performed essentially with their own body tools (hands to catch and fight, legs to run, etc.).

Here labour (L) leads directly to a product (Y):

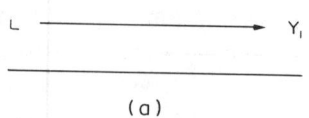

(a)

2. In the *pre-industrial*, essentially agricultural societies, more and more labour is devoted to the production of *tools*, which contribute subsequently to improving overall performance. These tools were of various sorts, e.g. the wheel, agricultural tools, bows and arrows, animal domestication, etc. and were developed and accumulated essentially without monetary investment.

---

[1] Table taken from *Dialogue on Wealth and Welfare, op. cit.*

However, more and more labour is already being diverted to an intermediary (indirect) manufacture of tools (P_c = cultural dowry and patrimony)

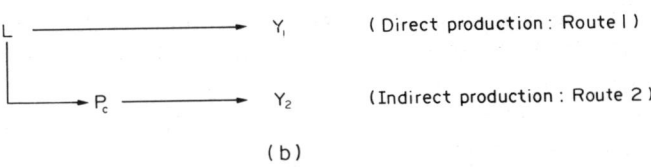

(b)

Clearly L will be diverted through Route 2 so long as the effort and resultant yield proves more satisfactory and sustainable than with Route 1.

3. In the *industrial society*, two fundamental events take place:

(i) Tremendous new developments take place in tool-making capabilities as a result of advanced and, subsequently, science-based technology.
(ii) The new technology needs unprecedented quantities of labour to be diverted from direct and traditional production. The accumulation of money (= Capital) is the way to solve this problem (and this is why, since the beginning of the industrial revolution, the *monetarised* economic system has grown more dynamic and potentially dominant).

The indirect production Route 2 next gives way to a new major bifurcation (3) leading to development of modern technology thanks to capital accumulation (C).

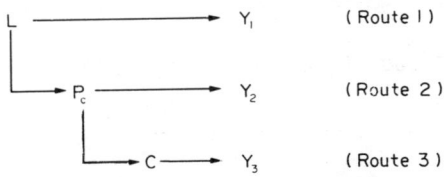

The greater the advances in technology, the greater the need for capital, so that:

In the eighteenth century, capital investment in the "modern" sector represents about 5% to 6% of sales.
In the nineteenth century goes up to 12% to 14%.
In the twentieth century goes up to 25% and more.

Currently, a single "machine" will increasingly cost over 1 billion dollars (such as a nuclear reactor of an offshore oil rig).

Obviously L will also continue to be advantageously diverted to Route 3 (increasing the capital intensity of the economy) so long as its efforts and yields prove more satisfactory and sustainable than in the case of Routes 1 and 2. In such evaluation, the increasing costs of coordination and management must also be taken into consideration.

4. In contemporary society, capital needs are related to:

 (i) Replacement of worn-out capital equipment (i.e. the situation in an equipment state economy).

 (ii) Investment in advanced technology, which makes existing equipment obsolete and allows a real net increase in productivity. This has been the prime growth factor of the Industrial Revolution. If technology is in a period of diminishing returns[2] and capital tends to have a low or even negative rate of return,[3] real yields will not improve by developing capital intensive projects. Direct human labour can then again become "competitive" in real-wealth production.[4]

 (iii) Geographical spread of investments, in particular where the limits of (ii) have not been reached and where other development factors (cultural, political, organisational) can profitably assimilate and benefit from the technological–industrial revolution on the basis of real utilisation value.

---

[2] Giarini, Orio and Loubergé, Henri *The Diminishing Returns of Technology*, Pergamon Press, Oxford, New York, N.Y., 1978.

[3] Kristensen, Thorkil *The Nature of the Present International Crisis, op. cit.*

[4] Vester, Frederic *Ballungsgebiete in der Krise*, Stuttgart, 1977. Vester shows that in Germany, 100 billion marks investment have "produced" employment for an additional 2 million people in the period 1955–60, 400,000 in the period 1960–65, *minus* 100,000 in the period 1965–70, *minus* 500,000 in the period 1970–75. In terms of "real" wealth produced by the apparent increase in capital productivity, one has to deduct the costs of Government subsidies, taxes and social security expenditures necessitated by the readaptations. See also the other tables and discussions on "value".

A New "Supply Side" Economics: The Question of "The Diminishing Returns of Technology"[1]

The assessment of the role of science and technology in the present phase of the industrial revolution is an essential question. The phenomenon of "the diminishing returns of technology" can be summarised as follows:

(i) Technological, usable knowledge has been accumulating during the 200 years of industrial revolution, at a speed which was often greater than the ability to use it. Many delays in the process of putting technology to use were of a cultural rather than of a technical nature. Inventions have often been available for a long time before their economic application has become obvious: entrepreneurs had to learn that science could produce something other than theories. Up until the twentieth century, technological possibilities were *de facto underestimated*.

(ii) This situation created the impression among economists that technology was adaptable at will. Their main concern became the management of demand. "Keynesianism" could work, because "supply" (thanks to a long-term factor!) was elastic enough.

(iii) In *recent decades*, through the professional organisation of research, possibilities for new technology are researched and tested almost in real time. The delay due to a lack of understanding of available or adaptable technologies is reduced almost to zero. Paradoxically, just because we are less ignorant, we now sometimes have the impression of being less powerful!

(iv) In fact, the delays in technological development are now more and more of a *technical* nature. The more complex and advanced the technology, the more time is needed to make it properly and economically viable.

(v) Furthermore, modern technology often depends on fundamental research, which carries the constraint of still longer delays (in the order of decades).

(vi) And thirdly, the more complex and advanced the technology, the

---

[1] See also: *The Diminishing Returns of Technology*, Giarini, Orio and Loubergé, Henri, Pergamon Press, Oxford, 1978. French edition: Dunod, Paris, 1979. Italian edition: Mondadori-Est (La Delusione Tecnologica), Milan, 1979.

more its direct and indirect negative aspects, together with its positive ones, have to be taken into consideration.

(vii) All this means that whereas the classical period of the industrial revolution was a period during which technology could in many cases have done even more than people expected (we were in a period of *increasing* returns of technology), the increase in scarcities in the world today is not matched by a technology which at least maintains economic costs at the same level, in the key strategic sectors (like energy).

For example, when oil has to be extracted from the North Sea, where it is more difficult (costly) to obtain than in Saudi Arabia, new technologies are not rapid enough to compensate fully (in economic terms) for the harder conditions of extraction. Technology is not able today to provide alternative sources of energy at lower costs and as rapidly as public opinion (and economists) hoped in 1973 and 1974.

We are in a period of diminishing returns of technology, which is nevertheless still different from a situation of *negative* returns of technology.

The situation of diminishing returns of technology also explains why from now on *supply economics* will be the key road of economic thought. Some American economists speak today of *supply economics*, in order to underline the necessity to diminish institutional constraints to investment, which are supposed to have a determinant effect on the entrepreneurial willingness to take new risks.

We believe that the explanation of supply rigidities by institutional causes is very partial: and in any case insufficient. Supply economics problems have to do not only with institutional constraints, but even more with:

(i) the diminishing returns of technology; and
(ii) the non-monetarised constraints (environment), which are so largely discussed in this report.

Furthermore, a consistent view of *supply economics* presupposes a new notion of value (whereas all views of neo-classical and Keynesians economists are based on a demand-oriented notion of value), which is also supply-oriented.

Economic Crisis, Interest Rates and the Diminishing Returns of Technology

The oil crisis of 1973 showed up the consequences of an economic phenomenon which started to be perceptible during the sixties: an increasing trend towards diminishing returns of technology. It is now becoming accepted that we have since been undergoing a structural economic crisis: sooner or later we shall have to find out the exact extent of the diminishing returns of technology and consequently of the increasing rigidity of supply in the triggering of this crisis in order to obtain a better understanding of the true economic effects of the proposed solutions.

Since 1973, and for many years, however, there have been strong attempts to believe that this was a simple crisis in the business cycle, which only needed to be overcome in order to return to what is considered "normal" growth. On this account, we have increasingly been faced with:

(i) an increase in the budget deficits of the various states and public institutions:
(ii) compensation for reductions in demand by state intervention in the form of "deficit spending";
(iii) compensation for the increase in power costs by agreements to guarantee real salary increases.[1]

During the same period, the balance of payments of many industrialised and developing countries has shown steadily rising deficits. All this has brought about an aberrant situation for the following reasons:

There has been and still is a falling demand for capital in most industrial and productive sectors as compared with the past, except in certain fields (e.g. energy, where the demand for investment, however, is highly uncertain).

The demand for the financing of deficits, however, both nationally and internationally, has more than made up for the drop in the demand for investment in production; indeed, we have seen and are seeing a

---

[1] This is, in any case, the policy followed in the Federal Republic of Germany, as explained by Helmut Schlesinger, Vice-Chairman of the Deutsche Bundesbank, Frankfurt, at the Alpbach Conference in August 1981.

demand for finance for consumption which far outstrips that for production. The latter does not have the dynamism which might justifiably have been expected, on account of the diminishing returns of technology.

The result is that, whereas diminishing returns of technology should entail a reduction in the demand for capital (and this was so until two years ago when the rates of yield on capital, taking inflation and taxation into account, were nearly always negative), this demand for capital is now highly excessive because of the call for finance for national and international deficits. Clearly, in such a situation, those holding the positive surplus are not very interested in recycling it to where there is a real need for capital. This has resulted in high interest rates, a situation which can only continue if spending and balances of payment go still deeper into deficit.

The policy of the central banks, however, is still to control the supply of capital by restrictive monetary measures in order to strangle inflation. It is nevertheless obvious that if the demand for capital is increasing on account of greater deficits, there is even greater pressure for high interest rates.

Finally, in the field of industrial production, interest rates can have only two effects: the multiplication of money markets outside the markets controlled by the central banks (whence an increase in the trend towards a semi-black economy here, too), and rising inflation owing to the repercussions on prices, costs and capital.

Today, therefore, we are faced with the practical consequences of the fact that, in the years after 1973, we refused to regard the economic crisis as a structural one, as the Club of Rome had pointed out and as is shown now by the analysis of the diminishing returns of technology. It will be all the more difficult to find a way out of the present dead end as we must also face the problems produced by the errors made in assessing the nature of the crisis reigning so far.

The great danger lies in the fact that interest rates, which in fact reflect tension between the supply of and demand for capital, but result from aberrant demand, may well imperil the entire financial system which may suffer major disasters in the short- or medium-term future. Likewise, inflation is less likely to be controlled (and may even not be controlled at all) as a result of the steps taken, but rather as a consequence of the excessive acceleration in the international crisis owing to the weight and distortions brought about by interest rates.

The main way out of this situation would be to give a frank explanation to public opinion of the *structural* nature of the crisis and its origins in order to create a favourable atmosphere for the political acceptance of a radical reduction in all forms of "monetarised" deficits, with a fair distribution of the burden of sacrifice. The Club of Rome's report entitled *Dialogue on Wealth and Welfare* provides a basis for a possible approach to this fundamental debate while permitting an optimistic view of the creation of greater "economic" wealth and welfare.

Index

Agriculture 52
  overproduction in 58–9

Biology 36
  research in 31–2
Biotechnology 32, 37
Bohr, Niels 55
Born, Max 55

Capital 17–19, 51, 73–4, 78
  accumulation of 73
  falling demand for 77–8
  life cycle of 11–12
  overcapitalisation 7
Capitalism 59
Cartesian concepts of science 53, 56
Cartesianism 60–1
Class struggle 19
Club of Rome 43–5, 68–70, 78–9
Consumption 78

Deficits 77–8
Deflation 15, 58
Descartes, René 21
Developed countries 31
Dowry & Patrimony (D & P) 66, 73

Ecology 47
  economics of 46–7
  movement 47
Economic
  crisis 77–9
  depression 11, 18–19, 34
  development 36–7, 51–2
    from 1945–70 39
  expansion 12
  growth 15, 31, 34, 36, 45–6
    limits to 44–5
  long-term movements 4–39
  policies 37–9, 72
  theory 42, 53, 56, 59, 63
Economics 47–9, 51–6, 59, 61–2
  ecological 42, 46
  and the individual 13

Keynesian theory 23
  post-industrial 59
  supply 76
Economy, the 47–9
  tertiarisation of 36
  updating of 43
Einstein, A. 54
Electronics 36
  micro- 31
Employment, problems of 68–72
Encyclopaedia Britannica 60
Energy 44, 47
  alternative sources of 76
  production of 44
  rising costs of 30
Environment 76

Fiscal policies 69, 72

Germany, Federal Republic of 77
Great Britain 34
Gross National Product (GNP) 41, 45, 47, 64–5

Heisenberg paradigm 55
Hirsch, Fred 64

Illich, Ivan 49
Industrial Revolution 34–5, 37–8, 42, 45, 48–9, 51, 59, 61–2, 64, 68–76
  and deflation 58
  life cycle of 17–28
Industrial society 68, 73
  post-industrial society 70–1
Industrialisation 26, 42, 48–53, 59, 61–3
Industrialised countries 45, 62, 64
Industry 22, 30–2, 36, 48
  specialisation in 25
  and the Third World 31
Inflation 1, 14–15, 58, 78
Information revolution 36–7, 39
Innovation 6–12, 18–21, 25, 27, 29–31, 33–5, 38, 42
  social 37

Interest rates 78
Internalisation 65
Investment 11, 19, 45, 68, 74

Keynes, John Maynard 35
Keynesianism 38, 58, 64, 75–6
   precepts of economic policy 35
   theory 23
Kondratieff, Nikolai D. 2, 4–5
   theory of economic cycles 2, 4–10, 12–17, 31, 33
Kuznets, Simon 65

Labour 72–4

Market/s
   free 54
   multiplication of money markets 78
Marshall, Alfred 48
Marshall Plan 35
Marx, Karl 18, 24, 50
Marxist
   philosophy/analysis 13, 17
   explanation of long-term economic movements 17–19
Monetarisation 28, 49, 51, 59, 61, 68, 72
Monetarised
   activities 66
   economic system 51, 73
   production process 63
Monetarism 38
Monetary
   economic values 62–5
   movements 12
   see also Non-monetary
Money, attitude towards 12
Morin, Edgar 43

New deal 35
Newton, Isaac 21, 54
Newtonian
   concepts of science 50, 55–6
   paradigm 54
Non-monetar(y)ised
   activities 66
   constraints 76
   economic values 62–5
   economy 63, 68
Nuclear fusion 32

Obsolescence 71–2

Oil
   cost of extraction 76
   price increases of 1, 30, 77

Pfeffer, Irving 56
Pollution 36, 44, 63, 65
Prices, shadow 50, 53
Prigogine, J. 55
Production 20, 59, 63, 68, 77–8
   investment in 77
   monetarised 50
   overproduction 22, 58
   social cost of 38
Productivity 38, 72
Products, useful life of 70–2
Profit, role of 38

Quesnay, François 48, 59

Raw materials, depletion of 71, 76
Research and development 24, 30–4, 37, 75
Resources, depletion of 71, 76
Risk
   analysis of 56
   institutions 59
Robots 37, 39
Roman Empire 49

Schlesinger, Helmut 77
Science 54
   Cartesian concepts of 53
   discoveries 21
   experimental 22, 35
   and industrialised countries 45
   inventions 35
   knowledge 23–4, 31–2, 34–6
   Newtonian concepts of 50
   and technology 23, 25, 29, 35–6, 44–5, 75
Scientific research
   Cartesian/Newtonian methods of 53–4
Sector/s
   service/s 36, 52
   tertiary 59
   monetarised 62
   non-monetarised 62
Service society 59
Smith, Adam 41, 43, 48–51, 53
Social sciences 55
Solzhenitsyn, A. 4
Supply, rigidity of 77

Taxation   69
Technical development/progress   11–12, 20–5, 29–39
Technological
  efficiency   42, 71
  revolution   18–19, 22, 59
Technology   23, 25–9, 35–8, 44–5, 48, 51–2, 73, 75–6
  diminishing returns of   25–9, 31, 38, 45, 63–5, 71, 74–9
  and long-term economic movements   33–7
Third World   31
Time, notion of   56, 65–6
Trade unions   19, 69

Unemployment   1, 5, 19, 39
United States   24, 34

Value/s   50–1, 53, 66, 70–1, 74

  added   57–8, 64–5, 71
  deducted   64–6
  non-monetarised   62–5
  priced   51
  theory of   48, 55–6, 59, 63–6, 76
  utilisation   66

War   5, 18–19
Waste-disposal   71
Wealth   51, 55, 58–9, 66, 71, 79
  distribution of   68
  of nations   50, 53
  real   46–7
Welfare   46–8, 51–2, 55, 58–64, 66, 71, 79
Work
  and the elderly   72
  part-time   39
  reduction in hours of   69–70
  unpaid   69, 72
  see also Labour